PROFITABLE PILATES

Everything
But the Exercises

Lesley Logan

TABLE OF CONTENTS

ACKNOWLEDGMENTS

There are coincidences...I want to thank those who got me into Pilates in the first place! The random suggestion from a friend's ex-boyfriend that we check out a Pilates class led me to my first Mat class in Orange County and it changed the course of my life. I had no idea how much it would change my world but that first class set me on a journey that has taken me to my destiny!

I also want to thank my family and friends who have been just as excited about the publishing of this book as I am. Thank you for your patience and support during the many unavailable Sundays while I wrote this book.

Thank you to the many teachers I have met that inspired this book. The struggles and consistent questions I heard amongst you all made me want to write this book even more.

A special thanks to Daniela Escobar who allowed me to see that I could be a Pilates Instructor and taught me every exercise I would learn in my program so I would be more prepared. Our friendship grew from the time I was your client to now as we are co-workers and you have always supported me and my teachings. Also to Carrie Macy, you have been a wonderful mentor and a very close friend. I am so thankful to have you a strong teacher in my life inspiring me to dig deeper into my own teachings each day.

Thank you to the many other teachers I have met that inspire me. Those of you who work for me and take sessions from me. The struggles and consistent questions I heard amongst you all made me want to write this book even more. Seeing your business grow and your Pilates knowledge deepen is so inspirational and rewarding. I am truly blessed.

Thank you to my dear clients who continue to grow within this wonderful method. Your accomplishments and dedication to your practice constantly inspire me and make me realize how lucky I am to do this as a profession. Thank you to Jeremy Brathwaite, Bonnie Silver and Mary Daily who answered interview questions that helped me make sure this book had the information Pilates instructors need. Thank you to Amy Taylor Alpers, Katherine Slay, Jeni DelPozo, Whitney Grafa, Kathleen Mangan, Lauren Berman and Rafael Romis for answering my interview questions and contributing your experience. Thank you RTF for your encouragement to start, finish and publish this book.

Finally, thank you to Joseph and Clara Pilates and the Elders who brought the method out to the world. Without Joseph's dedication to his method and the dedication of his clients I wouldn't have a profession to write about.

PILATES! It's what many athletes, celebrities and maybe even You and your neighbor rave about! Pilates is great for the whole body, the whole mind and even a great career. You don't have to be a lifelong Pilates client to become a Pilates teacher. Sure, it helps to have experience in it, but many great instructors started simply by signing up for a program and diving core first into a new career in Pilates. *Could this be you?* Before you run out and commit to this career, it's important to know the history, know what questions to ask and what it will take to be successful This is not your your guide to Pilates exercises. This is your guide to **everything but the exercises!**

Whether you know a little about Pilates or a lot, this book will help you decide where you want to go and the type of instructor you want to be. Dive in, read this all at once or if you're already certified skip around to the parts that will benefit your business today. Part of being an instructor is working with the body in front of you. This book will help you work with the career you have in front of you today, show you what you can work for tomorrow and be there in the future when you need a refresher!

CHAPTER 1

So you want to be a Pilates Instructor?

"Controlology {Pilates} is complete coordination of mind, body, and spirit. Through controlology you first purposefully acquire complete control of your own body, and then through proper repetition of it's exercises, you gradually and progressively acquire the natural rhythm and coordination associated with all your subconscious activities."

~Joseph Pilates

WHEN deciding if you want to become a Pilates Instructor it is important to understand what Pilates is, and where it came from.   Having an understanding of the history may help you decide if you want to be a Pilates instructor, but it will most certainly inspire you to be the best instructor possible.

Pilates, first introduced to the public in 1925, is a system of physical exercises, created by Joseph Pilates.   Pilates emphasizes mental and spiritual conditioning, to assist in strengthening the body.   Joseph Pilates believed in focus, breath, creating movement that required thought and control, assisting in the movement of oxygen throughout the body, bringing flexibility and alignment to the spine and improving coordination and balance.   **Movements are not always big, but they should always be precise and intentional.**

One of the unique qualities of Pilates is that it can be practiced on many different pieces of equipment, in different environments, with varied styles of teaching.   It was originally experienced on a mat, but developed into a system taught on machines, with pulleys and springs used for resistance training, or assistance, depending on the client needs.

So who can do Pilates?   EVERYBODY! Joseph Pilates believed everyone should be doing his work. It's not just for dancers or those needing to work on flexibility.   Whether you are young, old, fit, weak, tight, strong, it doesn't matter. The beauty of his work is its adaptability to each client's needs and goals.   Pilates is not a 'one size fits all" workout. You as the instructor tailor the method to the client in front of you. With very few limits on who Pilates is good for, it leaves a large market for you as a future teacher to take part in. There are lots of people out there who need Pilates in their bodies and you can be the one to introduce it!

CHOOSING the right teacher training program will be one of the most important decisions in your Pilates career. There are countless programs offered nation-wide and so many questions to ask. A few important considerations:

- Is the program you are looking at based on the teachings of Joseph Pilates? If you can trace the lineage of your teacher trainer back to Joseph Pilates, you are probably in the right hands.

- What is included in the training program? A basic mat certification is necessary for any level of Pilates teaching, but if you want to be more than a mat Pilates instructor, you will want to be trained to teach on basic apparatus such as the reformer, cadillac and wunda chair.

- Do you need to have taken a certain amount of Pilates sessions to enroll?

- How long will it take to complete the program?

- How busy is the training studio where you will be doing your apprenticeship hours?

- Does the teacher training program fit the style you've experienced? If you've been taking classical pilates, a contemporary program might not be the best fit for you and vice versa.

- What teaching opportunities do graduates from the program have? Some programs allow graduates to teach at the location, others might not have the space to hire every graduate.

- Keep cost and expenses in mind. Program costs can vary.

All these concerns and so much more will be discussed in the first chapters of this guide.

IS teaching Pilates lucrative? Before you begin a new business or career, it's a good idea to find out if it will enable you to make a living! The answer to this question is completely up to you. Your effectiveness as a teacher combined with your ability to "sell" Pilates to your potential clients will be the recipe for success. Where and who you teach are also factors in this equation, as well as your ambition and investment in your career.

Some questions to ask yourself or research could be:

- Where can you teach?

- Do you want your own studio or teach in someone else's? Will you pay them a rental fee or will they pay you an hourly rate?

- What is your own financial bottom line? How much do you need to make and how much are you willing to teach?

PILATES teachers can make anywhere from $17.50 an hour to $200 an hour, depending on the type of session, environment, and client. It is a huge salary range. Part of the goal of this book is to help you as a prospective teacher discover where you might best feel at home not only as a teacher of Pilates, but also as a business person, comfortable with the financial aspects and personal requirements of devoting oneself to this profession.

In the beginning of this career, it might feel like there will be a lot of money going out before any money comes in. Don't let that stop you! You will be learning an amazingly vast method that transforms people's lives and will most likely transform your own life, too.

IF you can approach Pilates as a business and have awareness of your own monetary needs, there is no reason why you can't make money. Whether you want enough money to just break even or want to be rolling in the dough is up to you.

As Pilates becomes increasingly popular, and more people are made aware of it's benefits, the opportunities for Pilates teaching careers is expanding. Up until the last few years, one could only experience Pilates at private Pilates studios, that were few and far between, and mostly in metropolitan cities. Now, you can find Pilates almost everywhere. Fitness facilities have added Pilates to their group fitness schedules. Some high-end gyms have even built full Pilates studios within their properties. Many dance and yoga studios also offer Pilates mat classes. Cruise ships have added Pilates equipment to their list of on-deck activities!

If you are someone who is trained in Pilates, and is comfortable in an office setting, the doors to a career working in physical therapy or a medical office are open for you. Pilates is being actively used in hospitals, physical therapy practices, chiropractic clinics, sports injury rehabilitation centers and athletic training facilities. The benefits of this are that you the instructor, have a relatively set schedule and the office books the sessions. If you like the security and schedule of the 9 to 5 life, it's still available!

Over the last century, Pilates has come a long way from Joseph's studio on 8th Avenue in New York City. Joseph Pilates hoped for his work to be experienced and practiced by everybody, everywhere. With the help of devoted teachers, and the popularity of celebrities and top athletes crediting their toned, lean bodies to Pilates, his work is more popular than ever.

Your Pilates career is waiting for you.

From Amy Taylor Alpers, a teacher of 23 years: "Have a personal Mission of exactly what it is that you want to accomplish as a Pilates instructor and always be on your own path to healing yourself through Pilates."

CHAPTER 2

You Oughta Know

"Since we are living in this modern age we must out of neccesity devote more time and more thought to the important matter of acquiring physical fitness."

~ Joseph Pilates

SO you want to be a Pilates Instructor? Fantastic! Knowing the exercises is just part of being an instructor. **A large part, yes, but not the only part.** Having the history of Pilates in your brain will help you answer questions from future clients and get you inspired to keep the method going! Do you know about Joe and the history of the method?

Believe it or not but many people still do not know that Pilates was created by a man! Joseph Pilates was born in Monchengladbach, Germany in 1883, to a gymnast father and naturopath mother.

Joseph was very sick as a child, suffering from rickets, asthma and rheumatic fever. To overcome his illnesses, he focused on strengthening his own body, mastering his breath, through yoga and martial arts. As a teenager, he was in such exceptional physical condition that he was a model for anatomy pictures. In 1912, he moved to England after having worked as a bodybuilder, a diver, and a gymnast. Once he arrived he became employed first as a boxer and circus performer, and then with Scotland Yard to assist in training police officers.

Once World War One began, he was interned in several camps with other German Nationals. At those camps, he began to teach a new method of exercise to the other internees, and bragged that their strength would be greater after the war than preceding it. He was creating his own style of fitness, based on his knowledge of anatomy, dance, observed animal movements and yoga, to instruct on the breath. If you think about the different activities in which Joseph Pilates excelled, they are all very focused on the breath, and as a former asthma suffer, Joseph recognized to not breath properly is to propel the body towards illness. At that time he was not only doing his original mat exercises but also designing pieces of equipment that he could roll over patient's wheelchairs or hospital beds. Joe called his technique **Contrology.** His exercises, now internationally known as "Pilates," require you to pay attention to exactly **what body part is moving** and to have a controlled intention as to **where is it going,** hence Contrology.

In 1925, Joseph Pilates moved to the US and along the way he met his wife Clara. Together Joe and Clara opened the first "Pilates" studio in New York City. They both taught the Contrology method for almost 40 years. In the early years of the studio, in addition to "regular" clients Joe and Clara also catered to some of the most famous dancers in the world, Martha Graham and George Balanchine included. His studio became the place where many dancers were sent to the studio to be "fixed." The combination of stretching and strengthening, with the focus on exercises that emphasize balance and coordination, were ideal for a dancer and any athlete or person that is looking to improve their fitness and protect themselves from future injuries and ailments.

Joseph and Clara would personally teach the new students that came to their burgeoning studio, in private sessions.   But once a student understood the order of work, and was able to complete the exercises on their own, Joseph and Clara would simply correct as needed, leaving a student to refine their focus without overbearing instruction.   Occasionally a new exercise would be added to the routine.   Examining Joseph Pilates' preference for solitary sports; diving, boxing, yoga, and dance, one can make the assumption that he believed it was up to the individual student to push themselves mentally to improve themselves physically, and his exercises were all one might need to be in the best mental and physical shape possible.   There are many quotes from him that also claim that practicing Pilates would make a person "happier," whether that would come from better physical health, or clearer mental health, one can only draw their own conclusion.

Joseph Pilates was such a believer in his methods he wrote to President Kennedy about putting his method in schools across the country.   He wrote two books, "Your Health" in 1934 and "Return to Life Through Contrology" in 1945.

Joseph Pilates passed away at the age of 83 in 1967. Clara and her niece continued teaching his work as did many of his students, known as the Elders.

THE Elders were the first people to learn and teach Joseph Pilates' methods. Each of his Elders has their own take on the method based on their experiences. A discussion of the Elders includes the following names:

- **Romana Kryzanowska** was a dancer, who became a disciple of Joseph, and eventually took over his Pilates Studio. She is one of the most popular teacher trainers of the classical method and many contemporary teachers even trained under her. You will most often see teachers list themselves as "Romana" students.

- **Mary Bowen** founded the Pilates Method Alliance, to create a system of national certification and teaches workshops each year there as well as continuing education. She specializes and lectures on the "Pilates Plus Psyche."

- **Robert Fitzgerald** opened his own studio in New York City and had a large following within the dance community.

- **Ron Fletcher** was a dancer for Martha Graham and opened his studio in Los Angeles. He is credited with bringing Pilates westward and introducing the method to celebrities and actors of the Hollywood community. His style of teaching is known as "Fletcher Work." A couple popular ideas that Ron Fletcher created are the Percussion BreathingTM and Fletcher TowelworkTM. Under his training you'll find a more contemporary approach to Pilates with a style that is all his own.

- **Eve Gentry**, also a dancer, designed her own "pre-pilates" method which is now known as The Gentry Method. She was one of the founders of the Institute for the Pilates Method in 1991. She was a believer in breaking down the exercise into "fundamentals," as the foundation for any Pilates movement.

- **Kathy Grant** was one of two students to actually be certified by Joseph Pilates himself. Kathy had a unique way of teaching Pilates with very animated descriptions to inspire the exercise.

- **Jay Grimes** continues to teach Pilates in Los Angeles. He is one of the few people that Joe Pilates trained to be a teacher of his method. Jay brings insight and perspective to his understanding and teaching of Contrology. Jay directs a teaching program for teachers at Vintage Pilates in Los Angeles, CA.

- **Bruce King** trained for many years with Joseph and Clara Pilates and was a member of the Merce Cunningham Company, Alwyn Nikolais Company and his own Bruce King Dance Company. In the mid-1970s King opened his own studio in New York City.

- **Carola Trier** was given permission from Joseph to open the first studio outside of Joseph's. She also underwent medical and anatomy training, and combined her medical and Pilates experiences to develop various exercises and stretching techniques for dancers, many of which are still in use.

- **Lolita San Miguel** was the other teacher certified by Joseph Pilates. Lolita was first an apprentice under Carola Trier, and later under Joseph and Clara Pilates. She's been teaching Joseph Pilates' methods for over 50 years and currently has a Master's Program for certified teachers that have been teaching for 3 years or more. She is the founder of Pilates Y Mas, a Puerto Rican Pilates studio.

- Another name mentioned amongst the elders is **Alan Herdman**, a dancer from London who studied under Carola Trier and Robert Fitzgerald, and then took his information about Pilates and the method back to London, where he opened the first UK Pilates studio. He continues to work in the Pilates world, often with the Balanced Body equipment and programs.

THERE are two main categories Pilates instructors fall under: Classical/East coast and Contemporary/West coast. Classical/Traditional Pilates instructors teach the exercises in a standard order that does not vary from student to student. They are usually close followers of Joseph Pilates. Contemporary/Modern Pilates teachers change the order of exercise, as well as breaking down each exercise and creating variations of the exercises and it's components. They may or may not be loyal to Joseph Pilates or any of the Elders.

After Joseph's death in 1967, the ownership of his studio changed hands a several times. With Elders teaching his methods around the country and the world, eventually one 'owner' began sending out cease and desist letters to many teachers, asserting that they could not call what they were teaching "Pilates" because he owned the name. Finally, a court ruling in 2000 found that no one could trademark the name, and "Pilates" teachers were able to breathe a sigh of relief and continue teaching Joe's method. But, since no one person owns the name it can be difficult to regulate the teachings and practice of Joseph Pilates as he intended. Today Pilates is being taught all over the world, bearing the name of the Joseph Pilates, but there are so many different styles of teaching out there! What kind of teacher will you be?

CHAPTER 3

Join the Program

"Contrology develops the body uniformly, corrects wrong postures, restores physical vitality, invigorates the mind, and elevates the spirit."

~Joseph Pilates

CHOOSING the right teacher training program will be one of the most important decisions in your Pilates career. There are many different kinds, varied styles, lengths of training, with assorted requirements. One studio may be a 3 month program but you have to do it 5 days a week, 8 hours a day, and you may not able to take 3 months off to devote to training. Another studio may run a year long program, with training only on weekends but maybe you don't want to wait that long to get certified. Some programs require a mat certification before any apparatus certification training is offered. It is really important to do your research and find the best fit for your life and wallet.

A pretty thorough checklist coming right up:

- **Is the program recognized by the Pilates Method Alliance?** The Pilates Method Alliance (PMA) is the international, not-for-profit, professional association and certifying agency dedicated to the teachings of Joseph Pilates. The Pilates Method Alliance was formed in 2001 as a professional association for the Pilates community. Its purpose was to provide an international organization to connect teachers, teacher trainers, studios, and facilities dedicated to preserving and enhancing the legacy of Joseph H. Pilates and his exercise method by establishing standards, encouraging unity, and promoting professionalism.*

- **Is the program you are looking at based on the teachings of Joseph Pilates?** There are many contemporary studios that are are forms of Pilates, but may not provide the classical repertoire. Many of the Elders, those original devotees of Joseph Pilates, opened their own studios, and have created something of a family tree. If you can trace the lineage of your teacher trainer back to Joseph Pilates, you are probably in the right hands. For example, Eve Gentry (one of the Elders) was one of the originators of what is now known as the Physical Mind Institute, which provides certification based on Joseph Pilates designed exercises, although the certifying studios are not PMA recognized.

- **Exactly what is included in the training program?** A basic mat certification is necessary for any level of Pilates teaching, but if you want to be more than a mat Pilates instructor, you will want to be certified in teaching on basic apparatus such as the reformer, cadillac, and wunda chair. There are many specialty pieces of equipment that are available in studios like the trapeze, ladder barrel and many props like resistance rings or balls. Will you receive instruction of these? Knowing the studios you want to teach in will help give you an idea of all the equipment you want to be trained on. If you don't know that answer yet, don't worry! Being trained on more equipment is better than less. It will give you more options for exercises should the studio you are in have the equipment, or one day you may decide to purchase your own.

- **What is required of you before starting the training?** Do you need to have taken a certain amount of Pilates sessions? Will they be teaching you anatomy, or do you need to be able to pass a basic anatomy test before entering the teacher training program?

- **How busy is the training studio where you will be doing your apprenticeship hours?** If a studio isn't very busy, it can make it more difficult to get through your hours quickly. The more clients that come to the studio allow you to observe all kinds of body types.

- **Does the course schedule work with yours?** Find out the days and times the studio is open. Are you able to get into the studio often? When is it busy? Is it busy when you can be there to observe? When can you practice teaching? Do these times work for your schedule? When will you have to meet for seminars? You want to make sure you have all the times, dates and hours required of you before you sign up and pay for the program. The simple and sweet of it: Are your schedules copasetic? Will you be able to get the most of the program with the current schedule you have today? Does the program have more than one location you can get hours from? Are the location/s convenient for you? You may be working around the full-time trainers, you may have to squeeze in teaching hours at 6 am, or 9pm, is it a location that is safe, are you able to get access if you are the first person to arrive at the studio?

- **How many other apprentices are in the program at a given time?** If there are 12 of you doing teacher training, and only 5 reformers in the training studio, be prepared for scheduling issues! If it's just you in the studio, who will you practice teaching on? What if you can't get volunteers for practice hours? Where will you get practice bodies from? Can you bring in family and friends?How does the specific program assist you in completing the requirements?

- **How many apprenticeship hours are you expected to fulfill?** 450-600 is typical. While that seems like a lot, you'll find you want every one of those precious hours to learn the concepts, techniques, cues and benefits of every exercise.

- **Does the teacher training program fit the style you've experienced?** If you've been taking classical Pilates then a contemporary program might not be the best fit for you and vice versa. If you find yourself drawn to a program different from what you've had personal experience with, be sure to start taking classes and sessions at the studio. You need to be able to teach what is practiced in that specific studio, so you need experience with their preferred style.

- **How are you expected to learn the material?** Do they have a manual? Are there textbooks, and workbooks that are suggested or required?

- **Is continuing education offered?** Many programs have workshops and specialty courses you can take after you have completed your hours.

- **Future Plans?** What career opportunities do graduates from the program have? Some programs allow graduates to teach at the location, others might not have the space to hire every graduate. If they do hire from within their training program, at what point in the program can you apply for employment? Some programs have clients you can teach and get credit towards your hours as well as getting paid or credit towards personal sessions.

- **Program costs can vary.** When comparing programs, you might find one that costs more, but you
get both mat and reformer certifications instead
of just one certification, in the same amount of
time.   However, the cost of getting certified is not
just the cost of the program. How many classes
and sessions you have to take before starting the
program? As mentioned before, some programs
require a certain level of previous Pilates experience, or private sessions with your master trainer
so your understanding of Pilates can be mea-
sured before your acceptance into their program.
Practice sessions during a program must be taken
into consideration.   Many programs offer a discount to apprentices. Some programs require you
to take at least one session a week with a certified
teacher, others require 7-10 self-practice hours
in a 5 day span. It's important to know what the
requirement and costs of each session are when
choosing a program.

- **Gas ain't cheap!** How much will you be driving to
and from the studio? Gas, mileage and wear and
tear on your car are part of getting certified. Clothing
costs, snacks or lunches while at the studio need
to be added to the budget.   What you might where
for a quick jog around the neighborhood is not
necessarily what you will want to wear, nor should
you wear while teaching.   Your clothing should be

form fitting, and made for body-conscious purpose and fitness intention.

- **Time is money.** You must factor in the cost of your time. You will be committing anywhere from 3 to 9 months to get certified. Can you afford that time? There will be occasions for seminars and/or tests where you may be giving up time at work, or giving up work completely. Do you have enough savings set aside to be out of work while you complete your training?

BEING a Pilates apprentice is much like being a full-time student.   Going back to "school" can bring on an array of emotions. While it's not a typical school, you will be treated like a student, have teachers, assignments and lots of studying to do. You will be a beginner again and you will be taught new things. While in your training program you will learn a lot about Pilates and even more about yourself.   Your strengths and your weaknesses will be highlighted, you will find out what makes you nervous, frustrated, inspired and excited.   Your dedication to learning will be tested. Allow yourself to be a student. Allow yourself to be teachable, regardless of your own Pilates or fitness experience.

Your apprenticeship is your time to observe, listen, try it yourself, investigate, and ask about anything you don't understand. Some things you may grasp quickly, some lessons will spark questions. Ask them!

Don't just listen and write notes and repeat. **This is your time to find out the why of what you will be teaching.**

While in a teacher training program, you'll have seminars where you will learn the exercises, the order of exercises, and how to teach them. You will be instructed about safety concerns and equipment guidelines. You will sit for lectures with your teacher-trainer, usually the studio owner or master teacher. This is your opportunity to actually learn exercises. There's a ton of information and it's impossible to absorb it all. Ask a lot of questions and take thorough notes. You may have weekly meetings with the teacher trainer. These meetings are a great time to go over anything you may have missed or feel unclear about from your lectures.

The bulk of your time as an apprentice will go to your "hours." These are comprised of observation, practice teaching and self-practice. Depending on your program, you may have anywhere from 450-600 hours to complete these hours are usually your responsibility to keep track of and get signed off. Most certifying studios have a system in place for recording hours and scheduling clients. If you are struggling getting your teaching hours in, talk to your teacher trainer and fellow apprentices. You may have an emergency or a family matter come up that you cannot reschedule. The more you devote yourself to fulfilling your hours as quickly as possible, the better chance you have to be prepared for any unexpected holes in your schedule Treat your apprenticeship and a full time job. Be accountable to your program as you would be to any other professional commitment.

YOU will be required to complete observation hours, which can be very informative, and useful for learning helpful teaching "language," and getting to see senior teachers at work. In the very beginning, just watch and allow yourself to have the experience of awareness, and practice "paying attention." Initially, you probably won't know what you should be looking for, but it's important to have a pen and paper at the ready. Take notes on the exercises, cues, the instructor's interaction with the client, where they stand, where to touch and anything else that strikes a chord with you. Some ideas to get you thinking:

- How does the teacher assist them into or out of an exercise?

- If the client is struggling with an exercise what other exercises do they give to help better prepare them next time?

- Did you like the teacher's tone of voice, or any specific wording? What cues worked or didn't work?

- Did the client have any injuries? If so, how did the teacher address it, and/or modify the exercise?

- If you are struggling with understanding a certain exercise, watch how a senior teacher works with their client.

- Observe how people move their bodies. What do most people tend to do? How does the teacher set up the exercise to insure the client moves from the correct spot on the first try?

After the session, reflect on the past hour and maybe you can answer some of your own questions!

KEEP in mind while you are observing that clients are not animals in a zoo. They are human beings, and your observing them should not take away from their session. Asking questions while they are in session is not appropriate. Talking to the teacher or student, or even an unrelated person in the studio can be distracting to them and their session. Eating and drinking in the studio can also be distracting to them and their session. You are not watching a home movie.

Next up, practice teaching on your fellow Pilates students! Don't freak out! You may have very little experience teaching anything, let alone Pilates. It's important that you practice teaching, even if it's awful. When you first start, it might be embarrassing, awkward, or frustrating. You might find it hard to not look at your manual when teaching. You might be wondering how you can teach and walk and talk all at once! In the beginning, it's all about just getting the words out. The way to success is through practice, practice, practice. The more you talk out loud, the more comfortable you will become. When you are doing your own workouts, whisper the instructions to yourself, you might get an odd look or two, but chances are your fellow apprentices will be doing the same thing. It's so helpful to let the other apprentices practice teaching you, so you can experience firsthand how important your tone, pitch, and vocabulary are to one's effectiveness as a teacher. Using a fellow student to try different cues, to see what works and hear yourself out teach loud, will make it less nerve racking to teach a real client.

SOME programs have rules regarding what apprentices should wear. Be sure to follow the criteria of your program.   If none is given, then dress as if you are an instructor already. Wear workout attire such as leggings or workout pants, workout top and sport shoes that are appropriate for a studio. Some guidelines to keep in mind:

- Beware that long pants can cause you to trip or get caught in the equipment.

- Tops should fit well but not distract from the work in the session. Revealing tops, "belly" shirts or low cut shirts can be distracting to your client. Exposed cleavage or midriffs are not appropriate in your new place of business.

- The studio shoes are important as a teacher because it keeps you looking professional and safe. While teaching, you might use your feet to brace against a machine, and being barefoot can feel vulnerable or leave you open to injury. Some studios require you to have a pair of tennis shoes dedicated to the studio that you leave there. This is a good idea for several reasons. You'll never have to worry about having the right shoes with you, and you won't track street dirt on the studio floor where you and your clients spend time.

- Jewelry should be kept to a minimum. You do not want your accessories to get in your client's face; this goes for scarves as well. Short necklaces and small earrings are ok, longer necklaces or bangle bracelets that make noise could be a distraction. Also, jewelry can tear the equipment!

- When working in such close proximity with others, keep your perfumes and colognes to a minimum or not at all. Though you may enjoy your delicious fragrance, not everyone shares the same olfactory joys. Also, busy and fussy hair, or overdone make-up is not appropriate either. Although it is important to be yourself, you must remember a Pilates studio is a place of business, with a focus on health. Coming to work unkempt or messy, smelling of cigarettes, last night's wine, or a particularly scented lunch are as unacceptable as they would be in any corporate office. You want to represent yourself as an ambassador of health and positive spirit.

ANOTHER set of hours that you must fulfill are comprised of self-practice. These are simply hours where you are practicing on your own, with or without a teacher. Depending on the program, you may be allowed to count the hours you let other apprentice teachers teach you, or you may be allowed to do self-practice as mat work at home. Check with your program and teacher-trainer what is acceptable. These are good hours to run through a whole workout, or just to master a difficult exercise. Sometimes these hours are best utilized by practicing whatever you have been taught in the most recent lecture, to make sure your practice is current to the material.

After you've completed a certain amount of hours you might be allowed to start teaching practice bodies other than your fellow apprentices. This can be scary at first, but remember the ultimate goal is to teach! Apprentice teaching provides immediate performance feedback, which is extremely helpful and necessary. Schedule these people as clients and treat their session as you would if they were paying customers. Keeping them on track with the practice as you practice teaching allows you to learn how to "progress" them as you will a future client. Don't throw advanced exercises at a beginner client simply because you need the practice or because you think they might be "bored". Practice teaching them what their body needs and working them towards their fitness goals.

Always stay on top of your required certification hours, making sure you are getting the balance of observation, self-practice and teaching hours. You should be doing self-practice hours throughout your whole certification process, even if you have fulfilled the course requirement. It is extremely important to have your own practice; try out group reformer classes, take a mat class at your regular gym or maybe you can get private sessions with your studio teachers at a discount. What cues did you like? Or what didn't you like? Did something new click in your body? Practice being a client so you can understand what your clients will go through.

As an apprentice you'll have plenty of information to study. Studying isn't always easy and for some, it may have been a while since you had to hit the books. It's important to set aside time to study not just the exercises but also anatomy, history of Pilates, the exercises, injuries and your observation notes. Take time in your studying not just to memorize but to ask questions and analyze. Does it make sense? Why does one exercise prep for another exercise on another piece of equipment?

Knowing how the body does and exercise will help you progress your client and protect your client. Sure you can memorize the bones and muscles but knowing the agonists and antagonists allows you to easily avoid contraindicated exercises and prepare for their future practice.

Planning ahead will help keep you organized with your hours, your studying and your life! Make sure to bring snacks and or lunch as you might not have time to leave to get something to eat. Bring food that you can quickly snack on in a break room or somewhere outside the studio, so you can keep on track with your hours and give your body fuel and nourishment.

Your body needs rests and so does your mind. A Pilates instructor needs to be present while they teach. So does an apprentice. This may be easier said than done when you have a pile of laundry, hungry kids, a friend's wedding or a job to attend to, but as long as you know to prepare for the time and energy required for Pilates program completion, you can ask for help and to ensure your own success.

Finally, during the certification process you'll be giving up a lot of personal time. You may feel frustrated that all of your free time is devoted to your training and you may get complaints from your friends and family. **Ask for their support during this intense period. It won't last forever!**

There is a lot of information to master, and it may feel like a huge challenge. But Pilates can be your gift to the world, to teach it as Joseph Pilates intended, and to put your own personal touch into your work. **Use your time as an apprentice to ask yourself questions, investigate what interests you.** Find a mentor to help discover the answers. Having your own angle creates the personal touch that will make you a teacher of the method and not just a repeater of written lecture notes. Your personal touch could become a niche all your own as you progress as a teacher.

"Most of us haven't been students for years. Learning something you don't know makes you vulnerable, especially as a grown person and you just sort of need to accept that. But it's also important to remind yourself it's not your whole life. It's easy to lose sight of that because it becomes all-encompassing as an apprentice. You're at a turning point in your life and that's challenging. Take time out, regroup and then get back in the game."

-Lauren Berman, newly certified

CHAPTER 4

Graduated! Now what?

"Patience and persistence are vital qualities in the ultimate successful accomplishment of any worthwhile endeavor."

~ Joseph Pilates

CONGRATULATIONS! By this time, you have completed your apprenticeship program. You are armed with the tools to teach the public. Or are you? There are a few more steps you need to take before you can teach the public. These are just the details. This is the icing on the cake. Don't let the small stuff keep you from fulfilling your dreams. The goal of this book is to help you be prepared for all the things you might need to know as your embark on your teaching career!

As a Pilates instructor you might need insurance; most facilities require their teachers to be insured, and it's wise to have it for your own protection. If you plan on working for a fitness club, they might not require you to be individually insured. However, if you work at a studio, out of your home, or rent space in a studio or gym, you will need insurance. Most insurance plans are billed annually. You'll want it for your own protection and the safety of your clientele. Once you are insured, you'll have the peace of mind of being protected from the "what if's." What if a client falls off a piece of equipment and seriously hurts themselves? What if a spring snaps while a client is doing an exercise? The safest teachers in the world cannot guarantee an accident-free teaching career.

If you plug "Pilates teacher insurance" into any online search engine, you will get a lot of different site listings. Make sure you pick one that is registered with the Better Business Bureau. The Idea Health and Fitness Association, www.ideafit.com, offers insurance policies through their website and offer policies for both mat and equipment teachers. The Alternative Therapy Professional Association, www.alternativebalance.com, offers different policies for students for $119, part-timers at $159 and professionals at $179[1].

Some fitness associations offer insurance discounts as part of their membership benefits, such as IDEA FitnessConnect and Pilates Method Alliance. Although they may have membership fees, joining these associations can expose you to different workshops and conferences for Pilates professionals. You may decide to join an association, get your insurance discounted through them, and use the association as a means to continuing education and networking.

It is important to research your insurance requirements, find the policy that is best for you, and feel like you have made an investment in your own career as a teacher, and in your "hire ability" factor, as well as having a safety net in place for any of the unexpected events that can occur in even the safest environments.

CPR certification is another necessity for you as a Pilates instructor! You never know when might need it, and it makes no difference "where" you might need it. If you are a teacher, you need the peace of mind that should the worst case scenario occur, you are trained to handle it. As a Pilates instructor, you'll be working with people of all age ranges and health status. Any number of things can go wrong, from an allergic reaction to a

---

1 prices reflect 2013 research

heart attack and if person needs CPR you need to be prepared. Most studios and fitness facilities have, or are required to have, a defibrillator (AED) on the premises. An AED or Automatic External Defibrillator can be used to help read a person's heart rhythm and send an electric current to help start their heart. When you schedule your CPR certification, make sure the class you attend offers the AED defibrillator training.

If you search www.heart.org, you can either enroll in an online course, or find an in-person class near you. The online course may seem cheap ($23) and easy, but your emergency won't happen online in the comfort of your home, so try to also take a class that will help you be most prepared in case of emergency, where you can actually hold and handle the AED device. The price of a CPR certification workshop is around $50, depending on the location and format. Most workshops are 2-4 hours long. You'll need to renew your CPR certification every 2 years. Studio owners and fitness facilities usually require this and will want to have a copy of your current card on file.

Knowing you are prepared to assist in a medical emergency is vital. Some emergencies are environmental, like a hurricane or earthquake; some are circumstantial, like a robbery or fire. If you work in a fitness facility or studio there should be an emergency plan in place. **When you are hired, familiarize yourself with the facility's exit plan...you never know when you'll need it.** Knowing where to exit in case of an emergency will not only get you out of the studio safely but also allow you to get your clients out safely. During their session, they are entrusting you with their safety, not just throughout the exercise, but throughout their scheduled time period.

If you're teaching inside someone's home, ask them what the emergency exit route is, or if they have an emergency plan in place. You might only teach them in one room of their house, and never see the rest of the home, but should there be a kitchen fire, you need to know the safest way out. If you're planning on opening up your own studio or teaching out of your house, you should have an emergency plan in place before you allow any clients to enter, and any teachers you hire should be familiar with the plan as well.

Along with knowing the emergency plan, you'll also want to know where to access a first aid kit. It's a good idea to have a well-stocked first aid kit for the little cuts and scrapes that can occur in an active day. Clients can even get stung by a bee on their way into the studio! They might not be able to have their session, but if you have an epi-pen available to someone with a life-threatening allergy, you may save their life!

Some clients, especially older ones, have thin skin and what was a dark bruise when they walked in, could become a cut the moment it rubs against a strap. A minor cut or scrape shouldn't end a session, having a first aid kit will keep you both safe and focused on the work at hand. First aid kits are easy to pick up and come in all sizes. If you are teaching in private homes or renting space in a studio, have a small kit in your bag in case one is not readily available. **Put a reminder note in your calendar every month or so to just check that your first aid kit is stocked.**

Once you are sure that you can teach safely, in any environment and under any circumstance, you might also be interested in exploring additional certifications or education programs. The Pilates Method Alliance, or PMA, offers a certification test regulated by a third party. The test is multiple choice and takes up to 3 hours to complete. You can take the test in person by paper and pencil, or by computer during scheduled testing times. Technically, what you receive after completing your apprenticeship is a diploma, or proof of completion. After you pass the PMA test you are considered "officially" certified, according to the rules of the PMA.

Currently, you do not need to be PMA certified to teach. The test is an extra cost; at the time of print it's $295 to sit for the exam. If you are a PMA member you get a 15% discount. The benefit of this particular certification is your participation in any PMA approved workshops or continuing education will count towards your certification renewal. Many programs require you get 15-18 continuing education credits every two years. You might be trained classically but want to take a workshop hosted by a contemporary program. If you're PMA certified you can count those workshop credits towards renewal. Perhaps the program you were trained in doesn't have any continuing education or none that interests you at the time. If you're certified through the PMA you're not limited to just the program you were educated through.

As you continue training, and begin your teaching, if you hear about ideas, specialties, or teachers that pique your interest, write them down. Keep a list of exercises, types of clients, equipment or just general areas that interest you. Sign up for mailing lists for workshops hosted by teachers that interest you. Take continuing education that gives you the information you need, to be the teacher you want to be.

Your first program is just your foundation. It's impossible to learn everything you'll ever need to know from one school, with a general focus. As a new teacher, you won't be ready to absorb much specialty education, and any continuing education might be tailored to your teaching location and real-world clientele. For example, if you teach only in an elderly care facility, pre/post natal info won't be necessary, but a Pilates workshop for hip replacements would be! Use your continuing education to hone your skills, refresh your mind, inspire your work and develop your niche.

Another continuing education option is a 'Masters' program. Elders like Lolita San Miguel and Jay Grimes offer Masters programs, as do a few other training facilities. These Masters programs are for Pilates instructors who have been teaching for usually 2-3+ years. These programs are more beneficial when you have a good amount of teaching experience. You will be able to bring a keener eye to observation hours, sessions and workshops. Like your first apprenticeship, these programs have hours to complete, seminars to take and teaching to do. Usually, the amount of hours is reduced and you are given a longer amount of time to complete everything. You may or may not choose to partake in a Master's program, or in any specialty training, but it's good to keep in mind as your Pilates career unfolds. Where you end up teaching, and who you end up teaching will inform your decision to continue your Pilates education.

You will also want to think about basic business supplies in the beginning of your career. You will need to update your resume, create business cards and think about the usefulness of a simple website or webpage.

If you work for a studio, fitness club or a doctor's office, they might provide you with business cards. If you are an independent contractor or work from home, you'll want to have cards that you can hand out, or give some to your friends, family or even co-workers to distribute. Your cards do not need to be fancy or expensive. On a minimal budget you can get 100 cards printed online for around $25 dollars or at local print shop. It's important to have something to hand out or leave behind so your contact info is available to potential clientele and contacts. Your cards should have your name, email/website, phone number, certifications and style of teaching clearly listed.

Creating a specialized email address, or setting up a separate voice mailbox just for clients can help you keep work and "life" separate. You might have a fun email like lesleylovescookies@hotmail.com, but having a professional email address like lloganpilates@me.com is more appropriate to use on your business card, or in any other business circumstance. If you can afford to set up a separate phone line for clients, do so, unless your friends enjoy hearing your cancellations policies every time they leave you a message.

Setting up a separate email is easy and generally low in cost if not free. If you already have an email account, check with your email provider how many free email addresses you get with your account. Usually you get 2 or 3 address per account, and more than that can be a fee of a few dollars a month, provided you keep it all through the same provider. If you have a website, you most likely have a webmail address through your site. For example, if you set up www.LesleyLoganPilates.com, the domain provider could offer you an email address like "Lesley@LesleyLoganPilates.com." If you have a smartphone, send that email to your phone, and you can stay in touch with all your clients and their scheduling with a glance at your phone. Most smartphones will even allow you to have a personalized signature, so you can have your policies, website link, or rates on the bottom of every email.

A basic website is useful because it's a great reference site for future employers and clients to get a better idea of who you are and your teaching style. A website address listed on your resume will be handy for employment submissions to fitness clubs, studios and offices.

A business card only has room for the most pertinent information, but a website is great to mention all the interesting and individual details about you, what you teach, your niche, and any continuing education you may have completed. A website also legitimizes your commitment to your new career. In this computer age, you will most likely be googled before any interview, so why not control the first thing a prospective employer might discover?

Your resume will need updating as well. Any Pilates teaching experience, as well as your training and certifications should be listed first, but you can also highlight any other fitness experience, sales positions or health care experience.

Your cards, resume and website have the ability to connect a possible client or employer with your name and purpose. Chapter 5 will go deeper into how you can use these tools for even greater success.

WHILE your first goal may be to get clients and or get a teaching job, it's important to understand some basic tenets. Clients are entrusting their bodies, their physical needs and goals in your hands. Before you go out into the teaching world, it's good to keep in mind some basic guidelines. The following are the Pilates Method Alliance Code of Ethics:

1) Do no harm

2) Teach within your 'scope of practice and give full attention to the comfort and safety of clients at all times
3) Maintain professional boundaries. The following constitutes improper behavior:
   Inappropriate physical contact
   Financial exploitation
   Sexual exploitation
4) Maintain client confidentiality
5) Direct clients to seek medical attention when necessary
6) Do not discriminate against clients or colleagues on any level
7) Do not intentionally solicit other Pilates professionals' clients
8) Treat clients and colleagues with respect, truth, fairness, and integrity
9) Comply with all applicable business, employment and intellectual property laws
10) Maintain professional appearance and conduct
11) Do not misrepresent skills, training, professional credentials, identity or services
12) Continue gaining education to enhance your skills and knowledge, and to provide the highest quality of services to clients
13) Maintain appropriate insurance (liability, studio, content, etc.)
14) Maintain appropriate teacher: student ratios in all class settings

THESE ethics were created so all teachers are playing by the same set of 'rules'. You may agree or disagree with the list. You might have some rules of your own to add. **It's a good idea to think about the ethics** ✂ **with which you want to conduct yourself.**   Ethics will protect you from blurring the lines. Chapter 6 and 7 will talk further about situations with which to prepare yourself. **For now, grab a paper and pen and write out your own personal teaching ethics.** Keep in mind how you would want to be taught and treated as a client. Also, think about situations that would illustrate the need for each of the above ethical rules. Is there anything you would add? Or maybe want to ask a fellow instructor about how to handle?   You might find that the studio, office or club you work for has a code of ethics. Be sure to ask your employer, make sure you're all on the same page. The more prepared you are for every situation and circumstance will allow you to relax and enjoy your teaching process, knowing you can handle anything that might arise.

As a Pilates instructor, one of your goals is to assist in guiding your client's bodies to an ideal balanced state. So, it makes sense that "do no harm" is the first tennant. It's important while we are working with clients who have aches and pains, to remember you are not a doctor. These are clients, not patients. Be cautious about any casual 'diagnosing' you may do. Have your clients seek out their own medical professionals if there is a medical question. It's also important that while you might have a favorite chiropractor or doctor or nutritionist, you encourage your client to research their own specialists. Although you may want to "share" a favorite herbalist, should your client somehow suffer harm through your referral, they can litigate towards you and your referral. If you're unsure an exercise is safe for a client, if they have a medical condition or injury, the safest choice is to skip it, until you can do research or ask a mentor if it's appropriate. When in doubt leave it out.

Protecting yourself and your business also protects your clients. **Be sure to have liability release forms for each client to sign before they workout with you.** If you're working for a studio or fitness facility they will probably have a standard liability release for your client to sign. Keep a log of the workouts your client does, this way if anything goes wrong you'll have documentation of the relationship, both physical and financial. It's better to have documentation than be empty handed in a worse case legal scenario. These client logs will be useful for other reasons and will be discussed further in chapter 7.

Finally, should something go wrong with a client, an accident, injury, or verbal or physical altercation, write down everything that happened. Contact anyone who might be involved, studio owners or your managers. Follow every protocol your employer requires to make sure everyone is protected, especially you. Before you begin employment, ask your new boss what the proce-dure is for such a situation. You might never need to put the procedures in place, but knowing what to do if something goes wrong will keep you from losing time and money in a litigation.

While you'll be bursting with energy to jump in and start teaching, remember these few extra steps you take for safety, can protect you and your clients, and might make all the difference 1, 2 and 10 years from now. You're creating the foundation for a long-time career. The stronger and deeper your roots, the further you can grow.

CHAPTER 5

Oh, The Places You'll Go!

"A body free from nervous tension and fatigue is the ideal shelter provided by nature for housing a well balanced mind, fully capable of successfully meeting all the complex problems of modern living."

~ Joseph Pilates

ONCE you have completed your program you can start sending out your resume! You might even already know where you want to teach. As a Pilates instructor, you get to decide how often you want to work and at how many locations. There are pros and cons to working at just one place, and also for working at a few locations. This chapter will take a look at the different places you can teach, the different roles you can play and some of the unique clientele you might encounter along the way!

One of the more popular choices for a Pilates instructor is to teach in a private studio. Private studios are usually opened by one or maybe two Pilates instructors or master trainers. The space is dedicated to mostly Pilates, although there might be a dance or yoga class offered depending on the space and available teachers. Private studios offer two options for employment as a Pilates teacher. You can be hired by the studio owner as a staff teacher, or you can rent space as an independent contractor.

When preparing for your interview, get some background info on the studio. What kind of teaching style do they advertise, what are the general hours of the studio, do they teach other things besides Pilates that you might have experience in? The interviewer will be interested in what else you can bring to the studio, just being able to teach the Pilates repertoire is expected.

When you go in for an interview, dress appropriately. You are applying to teach Pilates, so dress as though you are ready to conduct a session. You might be asked to teach a client, teacher or studio owner a partial or full session. Make sure you find out what kind of equipment the studio uses beforehand, and research the equipment. You can always ask a question if something doesn't look familiar to you, it's impossible to be 100% familiar with every style reformer, but if you are applying at a Stott studio, and have only worked on a Balance Body, you need to spend some time learning a Stott machine before your interview. Maybe go take a session somewhere on that equipment so you can get a 'feel' for it. Not only will you look more prepared for your interview but you'll also be less nervous to "performance interview" for your new job.

When you are hired by a studio owner, the clients belong to the studio and you are paid an hourly rate. The benefits of working for a studio is that you will have set shifts, and whoever does the scheduling or runs the reception desk will fill your hours for you. The studio does the advertising, and pays all business costs. The flip side of being a staff teacher means you will make less per session than if it was "your" client and if your studio is having a slow day, you might only get scheduled for one or two hours. If you are just starting out and trying to get your bearings, or have a another job, this might be a good way to get your foot in the door, and not have to worry about doing the advertising or legwork of finding your own clients.

If you work for a studio, your clients are not "yours." So you need to find out the protocol for

client logs. Client logs come in a variety of forms (see an example in Additional Material). They are similar to files that your doctor's office may fill out about your visit. They can be as simple as keeping log of the clients session dates, what new exercises they learned and things to watch out for, aim for or focus on next time. Some studios may even have logs that list out EVERY single exercise you could teach and you would check off the exercises you did as well as any notes for that session. If you go on vacation, or have a client that comes 4 times a week for lessons, and you only work two days a week your logs will insure that the client can continue making progress no matter who is teaching them. Everyone who teaches that client will know what their last workout entailed, and what things to be on the lookout for; it's a source of shared information, to keep the clients safety and progress a priority, no matter who the teacher is.

Typically, all the equipment at the studio is available for your use. If you have a special prop that you want to incorporate, get permission from the owner before bringing in equipment. Depending on the rules of the studio and their insurance policies, it might not be acceptable to bring in additional equipment. A fun thing to do is set up a Pilates circuit training class, where clients with some Pilates experience can rotate through the studio, doing a circuit of chair, cadillac, reformer, etc. Check with the other teachers and owner if this is something that would be allowed before taking charge of the space.

Every private studio is different. Each studio has their own rates and procedures. **Make sure you have, in writing, how you will be compensated.** Will it be for clients served or shifted hours? Additionally, make sure you know how often you will be paid and by what method.

When you work as an independent contractor, you are renting the studio space to run your business. The studio and teacher have a contract that states when the rent is due, and what you owe per teaching session. Usually rent is based on if the session is a private (single person), duet (two people) or semi-private (3+). The studio might also offer mat, reformer and tower class if space and equipment allow. The classes often have their own rental fee. As an independent contractor, you're able to control your own schedule. You also make more per session depending on how much you charge minus your rent. The trade for more money and freedom is increased responsibility for creating your own business. You will be in charge of your own recruiting, advertising, and selling classes and packages. The business side of Pilates becomes your responsibility when you're an independent contractor. If you are comfortable finding your own clients or prefer to be more "in charge" of your career, this option might suit you well.

SOME key steps to being in charge:

- When renting a space, the studio might have a general liability release form, but you might also want to bring your own, specifically naming you as a teacher, and keep it in your files, making sure you adhere to your personal insurance policy.

- You should keep your own client logs, and bring them to the studio, with your calendar available, so you can plan your next booking as you finish a session.

- Our clients should know what form of payment you take and most often clients will either hand you the payment before the session or after. You decide what way you prefer.Have your clients sign a check in sheet attached to their log. Bookkeeping will be discussed in greater detail in "The Price is Right" chapter.

- Always check with a studio owner before bringing your own equipment in. There might not be space for you to store anything at your rental studio, but if it's something small like therabands or weights it might be easy to just hand carry it in for your clientele.

AT either rental studios or staffed studios, you should ask about the cleaning policy. Don't assume some-one is going to clean up after you. Everyone is sharing space and equipment, so cleaning everything after use, putting away your props, and being flexible with available equipment is important. When you are renting space, your business will be even more successful when you are responsible for your own area, respectful of other's clients, and if everyone can safely and maturely work together.

If you're qualified, you might find yourself looking into teaching at a nursing home or other medical facility. Working in a medical facility or nursing home is similar to being on staff at a studio. Someone else handles scheduling, payment and client packages. The clients are already established or are coming to the facility for a specific reason. If the idea of advertising and promoting yourself, or the instability of independent contracting, worries you this might be a safe direction. You have a set hourly rate, you have set hours, and it is like any other 9-5 office job, except you are teaching Pilates!

Teaching positions at a medical facility might require more specialized training. Physical therapy offices see many clients rehabbing after surgery. Once a client can take their post-surgery therapy to the next level, your job will be to work their body like any other Pilates client but possibly with more modifications. The extra training might just be a few weekend seminars on post-surgery rehab or some facilities might require a physical therapy aide certificate. The continuing education means your level of expertise is greater, which increases your value in any locale. A medical office teaching job has other perks! Depending on the office, you might receive benefits, vacation time and even sick time. Some offices are just beginning to add Pilates to their medical "menu" but Pilates in a healthcare environment is growing in popularity--opportunities abound!

Another growing area for Pilates instructors is a fitness facility. Many specialty fitness clubs like Equinox or Gold's, not only offer mat classes, but have actual Pilates studios built inside the gym. One of the benefits of working in one of these locations is that all the potential clients are right there in the building! You can work with the front desk to coordinate your teaching schedule and availability and the gym will help advertise Pilates to their members. Many of these facilities offer health benefits, vacation time, discounts on sessions, a free membership and even a 401(k)! Your pay however is similar or less than working for a studio owner, but the perks are increased. A lot of fitness clubs have more than one location that you can teach at, or even transfer should you relocate! **Working at a gym offers the benefits of working for a company, but creating your own schedule.** Also, like a private studio the clients belong to the facility, they pay the facility, and then you are paid your hourly rate through a standard paycheck.

The personalities of gym clientele are often different from clients at a private Pilates Studio. Most gym members go to the gym, regardless of the availability or awareness of Pilates.   Clients at a Pilates studio are there for the specific purpose of Pilates instruction and training. A gym client might have a different learning curve, but they should be treated like any beginning Pilates student, and progressed in the same manner. An average gym member might not understand the method right away. They might be coming for just a "workout" and not see why precision and control are integral. They might just want the stretch or the core work. As the instructor you'll have to find the balance of "giving them what they want" and teaching them the Pilates method.

Pilates gains popularity because celebrities keep promoting it, crediting their movie-star physiques to Pilates exercise. Teaching a celebrity client has its own benefits and challenges. While they might share with the press that they are doing Pilates, it needs to be clear whether or not you are allowed to share that you are a their teacher! Just like any other client, privacy is important. They might not want the world, or even your most close-mouthed friend to know they take Pilates with you. There might even be a privacy policy, or non-disclosure agreement that you must agree to, before doing any teaching.

Celebrity clients might have you teach in their home. There are no rules about where you can teach, as long as the equipment is appropriate and well-maintained, and all safety measures are in place. Wherever you teach an actor, musician, or other person in the public eye, remember while they seem familiar to you, you are not familiar to them. Be as professional when teaching a celebrity as you would anyone else you instruct. The focus should be on their session, not their career, or your hopes for promoting yours.

Another thing to keep in mind is scheduling. Performers and people in the entertainment industry are often on the move. They might be working with you and also have a Pilates teacher in New York or London or anywhere else they might be calling home. You might want to find out what kind of Pilates they are doing, if any, while away. This way you can help them maintain their goals and body requirements. You might be asked to teach them on set. Keep in mind that their schedule might not be predictable and so a working relationship might require you to be more flexible. You'll have to decide how flexible you are willing to be.

Many personal trainers, yoga teachers, and Pilates instructors are hired to travel with a celebrity client. This might be enticing for you. Keep in mind that if you travel with them, you won't be able to build a business and you might lose some of your previously established clients. If you choose to base your teaching livelihood on just one person, enjoy your time with them, understanding that it can change at any moment! Every decision is a choice, so make sure you look at both sides of a very glamorous coin!

Celebrities are not the only people who have Pilates equipment in their home. As Pilates continues to grow, many people are making room for a reformer or Cadillac. Many condominium buildings and luxury apartments are equipping their building gyms with Pilates equipment. Teaching in someone's home is nice for them and can be great for you too. It gives your client the privacy of having a studio all to themselves and hopefully they continue their Pilates practice on their own in between your sessions. When determining your home teaching rate, you'll want keep travel time and mileage in mind. You might lose an hour of teaching time due to a commute. Can you make it financially worthwhile to teaching them in their home and still fill your studio schedule? This is a question only you can answer.

TRY to maximize in home visits:

- If a whole family is interested in doing in-home Pilates, you can schedule everyone back to back.

- At a condo or apartment building with a Pilates reformer in the building gym, perhaps you can get multiple clients in the building and try to schedule them on the same day.

- Find out if the condo or apartments have equipment or space for a mat class and talk with the property manager about leading some classes.

SOME other considerations teaching in a client's home:

- You might not have all the equipment you wish to teach on. They might only have a reformer and floor space. Can you fill the time and give them the workout they need and want with just a mat and a reformer?

- Is the equipment something you're used to teaching on? Be sure to find out what kind of equipment they own ahead of time, so you can decide if you want to bring additional props.

- At a client's home you won't have to share equipment with another studio instructor. Having the ability to take up all the space you want and talk as loud as you want is always nice! However, does your client have small children or animals that you will have to work around?

- Do you have allergies? In a studio you can guarantee that plants and animals are minimal if at all. When going to someone's home you cannot control animals, flowers or other scents that might bother you.

YOU can teach at only one person's home, or make your whole business based on being an in-home teacher! If you enjoy changes in scenery and don't mind doing a little driving, this option might feel like the best fit. There are many personal staffing service companies that hire out Pilates instructors for at-home instruction.

You may decide you want to open a home studio. If you're a stay-at-home parent, this might make sense for you. Scheduling sessions around your children, or spouse's schedule can be very convenient. You'll want to consider several things when deciding if this is the option for you. Do you have enough space for the equipment you'll need? Will you be teaching privates, duets or classes? The amount of equipment and space you have will determine what is possible. There are also many insurance liability questions that should be answered by your insurance provider before making a final decision.

OTHER decision making factors:

- This option might provide you with the most com- fort, but also the greatest expenses--you will have the expense of investing in equipment. You will be responsible for your own advertising and promotion.

- Do you live in an easily accessible neighborhood? Where will clients park, how will they enter your home?

- How much of your home will clients have access to, and do you want strangers coming inside? If you have a detached garage that can be turned into a studio, or a carriage or guest house with its own entrance and bathroom, then you don't have to be concerned about sharing your living space.

TEACHING at home allows you to control all aspects of your business. You are your own boss, accountant, cleaner, teacher, and studio owner--it's the good news and the bad news! The equipment, design, schedule and clients are all your choice!

Pilates is mostly done by adults but is appropriate for children, too. In fact in Joseph Pilates' book, "Return to Health," he talks about educating your child on proper movement. The earlier a child learns to move correctly, the less likely they are to develop poor habits and posture. The PMA has a program 'Pilates in the Schools' (PITS). If the idea of teaching children gets you excited, This program might be just for you! While young children cannot use equipment due to size and weight, the mat work is fantastic for developing balance, posture, and mindful movement. The PITS program is designed for middle school students, 5th and 6th grade, and assists the instructors to incorporate their program in local kid friendly places such as after school programs, the Boys and Girls Club, the YMCA or other appropriate venues.

Unless there is a private classroom in your Pilates studio, it might not be the best environment for a children's class. Luckily, you could teach a children's class in a park if you wanted! The important thing when teaching children is to keep it fun, keep the classes small and talk to them using exercise names they can relate to. Using Pilates is a great way to get kids excited about fitness. It's also something that you might be doing for little or no money, unless you get a job teaching at a summer camp, or private school. You might be volunteering your time in the beginning, but you never know what can blossom from a kind act. If you're looking for a way to stay inspired while teaching, it might be worth it to volunteer your time or offer a reduced rate to a children's organization like the Girl Scouts, or YMCA. If you have interest or experience working with children or adolescents, there is always a path for Pilates!

The great outdoors can be an enticing classroom for all populations, especially on a beautiful day! Teaching a mat class outside might be something you want to do for a particular season, or for an event or fundraiser. When teaching outdoors, keep in mind the amount of privacy you are trading for the pleasure of the environment. Teaching on the Santa Monica bluffs might sound amazing, but depending on the time of day you have bright sunlight, smog, bugs, tourists and cars to deal with. It might be perfect at 6am, but 6pm might be too hectic.

What equipment will you bring for an outdoor class? Are you bringing the mats or asking the clients to bring their own? What about magic circles, weights or other fitness props? Will you have enough to go around if it's a drop-in class? **It's a good idea to leave your business cards outside the teaching area in case an observer wants more information.** Bring release forms for all attendees; you are still liable as a teacher regardless of your teaching location. You might just teach private mat sessions outside during good weather. The change of scenery might give the session new energy. Teaching outside could bring a lot of attention to you and maybe attract potential clients!

You might enjoy traveling! You could teach on a cruise ship! You would commit to several months at a time and your clientele will change every few days to every few weeks depending on the length of the cruise. Whenever you travel to teach you want to keep in mind how much you need to get paid, to make up for any loss of established "home" clientele. A cruise ship might not pay as much as private clients doing studio rental, but if you don't have a set clientele yet it might be worth doing to gain teaching experience and have the opportunity to travel.

Maybe you are offered an opportunity to teach in another country for a month or so. You might lose a client or two but it might be worth it for the experience and networking! Teaching on the road allows you to get your name out there, teach workshops and experience conferences around the world! The most important thing to keep in mind when teaching on the road is that the more organized you are, the more you plan ahead, the more opportunities you'll have and the smoother your journey will be!

Wherever you decide to teach, it's not set in stone. Unless you sign a contract that says you are exclusive to one place or person, you can root yourself in one or multiple places. If you don't have the experience you need to teach at your dream studio, go teach somewhere else and come back! Your Pilates career and where you are the happiest in your work environment will change and grow as your teaching experience evolves. Try out different options; always weigh your pros and cons. What works for you might not work for someone else, but you have the luxury of discovering the place that fits your best style and life rhythm. Your teaching will be at its best when you're in a place you enjoy teaching.

"There are two things that I love about teaching. 1 is that it is endless education. I will never know everything and always learn something new every day which takes me to my second favorite thing... my clients!! I learn so much from them each day. Hearing their success stories with what I have taught them makes everything worth it."

~Jeni Del Pozo first year instructor

CHAPTER 6

Hi There, It's Me!

"The whole country, the whole world should be doing my exercises. They'd be happier."

~ Joseph Pilates

IF the words "advertising", "marketing" or "sales" make you nervous, or scare you away from teaching Pilates, take a breathe deep and relax. Starting a self-made business can be as big or small of a commitment as you desire, the fate of your "company" is in your hands, but try and see that as an opportunity for growth and freedom rather than a scary burden. This chapter is all about ways to market yourself, so focus on the ones that you think will work for you and your personality!

The first thing to do is create your "**Elevator Speech.**" You need a quick, concise one or two sentence explanation of "**What you do and why**?" You can find clients everywhere, and YOU are your own best source of advertising so be prepared anywhere...in line at the grocery store, during your own gym workout, trying on clothes, and of course, in the elevator...to promote yourself.   It may feel uncomfortable at first to just start talking to strangers, but really it's no different than beginning a first session with a new client.

The next time you are out and about, maybe at your local coffee shop, practice striking up a conversation with the person in line next to you. See how quickly you can insert that you are a Pilates teacher, and give your quick speech. See what happens! They might have heard about Pilates and want more information; where can they do Pilates, or how much does it cost? Get ready to give your name, your studio, contact info, and be enthusiastic! Speak with clarity and confidence. Excitement can be infectious. The more you get used to answering the most common questions about Pilates, you can get) your answers solidified and ready to deliver. The dialogue will not go exactly word for word every time, but having a good handle on some key phrases will help you feel more confident and comfortable.

An example might go like this:

"On your way to work too? So am I!" The potential client might say *"What do you do or where do you work?"* **Then here comes your Elevator Speech:** *"I'm a Pilates instructor! Have you heard of Pilates? It's amazing! It's the one fitness method that lengthens and strengthens at the same time! You don't need to be strong or flexible to get results-if you haven't tried it I'd love to give you my card or schedule a session."*

AND you are on your way to a conversation. You can use any opening sentence you like; you could talk about workout clothes, exercising in "this" weather, local businesses in your teaching area, whatever opens the door for your speech.

On a website or flyer, you can have your text exactly as you want it but you can't see your audience to be able to make it a personal conversation about Pilates. To make a personal connection, you'll want to tailor your words a little. For example, if the enquiring party is a man, it's a good idea to mention Joseph Pilates was a male, a boxer and/or emphasize the strength based workout that he created.   If it's a elderly woman, you could mention how Pilates helps with balance and posture.   If you're an instructor at a physical therapy office your speech will be more about healthcare and injury prevention or treatment. **Being able to quickly deliver "bullet points" about Pilates will help you spread the word about you and your teaching.** Pilates works on everybody so it's important to be able to have a quick reason of why it could help your potential new client.

Remember your speech is special to you, what you do and why you do it! What is it that makes learning Pilates with you unique? What sets you apart from the rest of the pack? What have your personal experiences with the method been? Write it down until it sounds quick and polished, and you can deliver it without pausing--but make sure it sounds like you, feels light and exciting! After you've given your speech, and maybe answered a question or two, if you managed to capture their interest they'll ask for your card.   If can, try to grab their card too so you can follow up!

Besides having your "elevator speech" at the ready, you should store cards and flyers in your wallet, purse or gym bag. Keep some extras in the glove compartment of your car. You never know when someone will ask for one! You are your own business, so take "yourself' with you wherever you go, whether it's the salon or the car wash. Flyers can be more detailed than business cards (discussed in the previous chapter), as you have more space to work with.

DEPENDING on your location and your teaching specialties you might want to leave cards and flyers around town. Where?

- If you teach pre/post natal Pilates, "Mommy and Me" style places are great spots to drop off your cards or flyers.

- Got Golf and Pilates knowledge? Drop off your info at the local golf shops, driving ranges and golf courses.

- Experience with runners, post your flyers at the run shops.

- Flyers can also be left at local coffee shops, community centers, on public bulletin boards, doctor's offices, under windshield wipers or on door knobs. Always use your discretion when you put up your flyers or cards. You don't want to litter the streets, be inappropriate, or waste time and money by putting them where people won't see them.

WORD of mouth advertising is still one of the strongest forms of gaining clients. Getting a personal recommendation from a friend or co-worker holds weight, because it comes from a positive personal experience. This is why giving great sessions every single time, no matter how tired or scared you are, is so important. If you only have one client a week but they are experiencing great results, their friends and family will take notice, and your client will definitely be talking about you!

WAYS to get people talking:

- Contact a local fitness store that will let you teach a class for their customers. This is a great way for people to see and/or experience what you do!

- Grab some close friends and teach them outside in a park!

- Volunteer to teach a class at a community center, or at a local community college.

- Teach a class as part of a fundraising event.

THE sky is the limit on where you can put together a quick class, and not only are they fun to do, but a great way to let your teaching shine, and spread the word about you! Ron Fletcher, a Pilates elder, never even published his studio phone number; his clientele was all from word-of-mouth!

A website is also a great way for people to "meet you." Your website is a great business building platform that can be as simple as a webpage with your contact info. A key component of the website is your actual URL or web address. It is a valuable tool to be able to say-"Oh, go to www.LesleyLoganPilates.com and you can see exactly what I do!" **A memorable, simple web address is invaluable for a burgeoning business.**

IF you are a beginning teacher a webpage may be all you need. GoDaddy is an excellent hosting site that will assist you in choosing a domain name. You can design it yourself. It should have photo of you, list your contact information and a description of your teaching with teaching locations. Anything else you want to add is up to you. Your website will grow with you. Your website doesn't need to include your rates; you can list any introductory offers at your discretion. To have a more interactive website, where you can link to your blog, or your social media, like Facebook or twitter, be prepared to make a bigger financial investment and hire a professional web designer. Videos, reviews and pictures make your page more unique to you and also increase the likelihood that people will spend more time on your site learning about you. Some other things to consider as you create your site:

- Should you decide to design a logo, keep it consistent. Use it on your cards, flyers, website, blog and/or other pages. This way, as people are doing searches, they become familiar with the logo, and recognize it as your signature image. Your logo is your idea. It can be a Pilates pose, it can be your face, it could just be your name in a special-ized font. Be as creative as you want, just keep it consistent.

- If you show pictures of others get their permission, and if you display photos of yourself make sure it is a good example of Pilates form. If teaser is not your strongest position, show standing side split. Whatever you choose, show the best version of you, and of Pilates. Pictures of Pilates give people visual reference for the exercise. Many people have heard of Pilates but they think it's like yoga or have no idea what the machines look like. Show them!

- Triple check for errors and correct links.

- Whether you create a webpage or a full website, make sure you are promoting the web address, or URL. Put your information and web address in online directories. Add it to Yelp, the online Yellow Pages, and search out online fitness directories. List yourself on any "Citysearch" style websites and participate with any review-based directo-ries. Put your web address as part of your email signature, and make sure it is on any business card or flyer you choose to hand out. Your web address, and its visibility, will create your online word-of-mouth.

- An email capture is a great way to get potential client info an email capture is a place on your website that allows a potential client to give you their info, name email phone number, fitness goals and experience and any other info you may wish to have. They can give this in exchange for free videos or to get you to contact them

- People have to be able to find you. Having popular "search words" in your URL and on your web page is the best way to gain attention on the web. The more your name or studio name appears during an internet search, the more likely people will look at your site. Having popular search words in your URL, site and/or pages means your info pops up more often or higher up in a search list. You might be competing with popular fitness websites that pay for the top spots but your page can come up just as much as their does without you paying for those spots. The more a potential client sees you when they search the more likely they will click on your site!

- If you choose to write a blog, and link it to your website, you increase the chances of your website coming up in a "Pilates" search. When you update your blog, it creates a "timestamp", and the most recent website comes up first in a search. If your blog is on your site, your webpage gets the benefit of increased traffic. Blogs are free, it can be fun to play around and read other people's blogs, and if you comment on a blog, leave your URL with the comment. You can find fitness groups online, and start networking within an online community. Take advantage of the World Wide Web and see how far you can cast your net.

- It is not absolutely necessary to have an "app" for your studio, but clients need access to you and your services online, often at non-"business" hours. The way people interact has changed. The majority of the Pilates market is women, and they are also the leading group of purchases of wellness/fitness apps for their tablets or smartphones. People are looking to schedule, pay, and book online. If you work for a studio, take note of the online system they use, and think about if that is something you want for yourself, should you go freelance, or have your own studio in the future.

- Creating a website brings with it a commitment to keep it updated, current, and a great representation of you. This is often your first impression on a prospective client, and you want to make sure it's informative, exciting, and enticing!

F the idea of self-starting a website is too much or too far out of your technological comfort zone, you can always hire a web designer to get you started. Web designer Rafael Romis was invited to give some feedback regarding this potential client-designer relationship.

"For an average Pilates website with no advanced features like booking classes and the sort, the price may range from $500 to about $5,000. More specifically, you could get someone to customize an already-designed template (which would not be unique to you) with your information for under $1,000 or you could hire someone to create a unique made-for-you website which would generally cost $2,500+. Note that these are freelancer prices - an actual web design agency would most likely charge north of $5,000 for anything. $1,000 is a good price to fully customize an already-designed template and $3,000 is a good price to make a custom website with a unique design - the client would get a website in both cases, and while the one is 3x the price of the other, they really are both good prices. People should talk to their web person and they should hire someone that they like working with. One of the most important things is communication and you want to make sure that the person you hire is someone that will work with you to achieve the best result and that doesn't just see you as a quick payday. You should look at their portfolio and then talk to them, go over things you like, ask for their input…see if you are on the same page. Don't just hire someone because they just have a great looking portfolio or their price is cheaper than the rest because like everything else, you get what you pay for. If I were to build my own "website" using user-friendly tools that most people would be able to use, it would take me 30 minutes. The first time I did it, it took me 2 hours. If I didn't know anything about websites, it could take me a day. If I didn't know a lot about the internet, maybe a few days. They say that a website is like your online business card. I say that it's much more than a business card. Nowadays, 90% of people will Google your name before they buy a service from you. That's 90% of your potential clients. Do you want them to see a website that's not going to look professional? I know I wouldn't. It would make me look bad and/or sloppy. For someone who cannot afford to hire a web person for their site, I would recommend holding off. A Facebook page will include all the information they need to see and it will probably look decent too." Rafael is available to be reached through his website www.weberous.com.

Social marketing has become widely used in the business world and can be a great marketing tool for a small business. If you don't have a Facebook page, get one! 53% of the population uses Facebook ! There is a difference between a profile and a page. To have a page you must have a profile but your personal profile can be as completely private while still keeping your "page" viewable to all. A profile allows you to 'friend' people, and you are limited to the amount of friends you can have. **A personal profile with your friends posting pictures and comments is not always appropriate as a business tool while a Facebook page is viewable for people who may or may not already belong to Facebook is great for your business.** A Facebook page is public and allows clients to "check in" when they are taking a session with you! It also lets you write status updates or create events just like a profile does. People can "like" your page, and this will allow them to get updates on your new classes or anything else you might want to share about you and your business. Its online grassroots advertising: if you get one client to like you, their friends see your page, and hopefully one of them will like you, etc. You can start reserving and branding your name and/or business name on Facebook even before you get a website up since it's totally free.

If you want a low cost way of advertising yourself Facebook ads might be good for you. While these are not free, you can set a daily budget or bid on a cost per click. Keep your target market in mind when making social media decisions; will your ideal clientele be

Facebook users? Facebook ads can be tailored to specific demographics. If you know who your audience is, you can tell Facebook whose news feeds should include your ads. If you're an instructor in Illinois you can make sure only users in your local teaching area receive your advertising. This puts your dollars to work the way you want them to. Your ad can be just about your page, can be an event promotion or even a link to your blog post.

Twitter is another great way to connect and announce updates about you and your teaching career! People can follow you and if you're adding a new location or class, it's an easy option to get the word out! Get a Twitter handle even if you're undecided, so you can keep and reserve your business "name." The best times to post if you want something to get the most attention possible is during the beginning of the week, from 10am to 1pm. If you want something to go viral save if for the beginning of the week not the weekends and remember tweets only last about 2.5 hours. Tweets are best for last minute deals or class announcements. Use Facebook for posting blogs and interacting with pictures and comments. There is a social media scheduler called Hootsuite, where you create all your tweets, Facebook posts and blog entries during a convenient time for you, then schedule when you want the app to post for you during the ideal time for social media exposure.

Linkedin is advertised as the more "professional" social working option. Since it's free to join you might consider it as a way to meet other Pilates professionals. Just like the word of mouth of your clients, knowing other Pilates instructors is useful. They might send you referrals from a different state, or send you specialty clients they cannot teach. A benefit to using Linkedin is their recommendation feature. The more recommendations you get from Linkedin users, the more your credibility can increase.

There are other online social networking options that allow users to find you, rate you, and "check-in" with you. When a client "checks-in" on their social media site, it shows the world they are taking Pilates with you, like real-time advertising! Your clients can be your best billboards! Encourage loyal clients to check in on Yelp, Foursquare and Facebook--they can help build your business just by showing up! Depending on where you live and work there might be another forum that people use more. Be sure to pick the most popular option. If you're new to the "check in" idea, ask around, see what other teachers might use, or what your friends or clients are comfortable with. You never want clients to feel like you are using them for free advertising so maybe you offer a discount for every 15 check-ins or have a "check in" contest!

YouTube channel allows you to post videos of you doing what you do best! So grab your camera phone or a real camcorder, teach and upload your video to YouTube! You can teach or demonstrate anything you want, and it allows more people to find you, see you and get to know you. As a Pilates teacher, if you can connect with people, they are more likely to trust you with their bodies and are more willing to build a teaching relationship. Just like your elevator speech you'll want to keep all your online options fresh, current, and professional.

Other options for advertising are donating gift certificates to a local auction; it's a great way to get your name out locally. The cost to you is your time for the session and any rent. But the winner isn't the only person who will see your name and info! Every person who bids will see it too!

Daily deals are another form of marketing where people buy a session or package at a discounted rate (usually half off) and you split the amount they pay with the host site. Again, just like the donations people who don't buy your deal will see your info as well! It's another way to get you out there. This book discusses discount-style marketing in Chapter 9

IF you decide to do social marketing keep in mind a few tips:

- Make sure you're representing your business appropriately and professionally. Once your information is posted, it's out there for the world and your potential clients to see! Edit and re-read and carefully think about what you're putting out there into the webisphere.

- Interaction is key! If people write comments, questions, reviews or emails, you should respond back promptly! If you aren't able to respond to people in a timely fashion, social networking might not be the best option for you.

- If you're not using it, close it! If you open a social marketing account and realize it's not the route you need, don't just leave it there. Close it. If you are not updating it, the purpose is not being served, and can even give the message that you are out of business or not interested in new clientele.

- Now that you have online fans and followers don't treat them as though they're imaginary. Make sure you check in. Ask them for input on a blog or what they would like for a video post? Keep them involved!

HOW you ultimately decide to put yourself out there is up to you! The majority of the population is online, but remember nothing beats a friendly in-person smile. Knowing who your target audience is will help you. Keep in mind who you are, and what you offer. Use social media to increase your exposure, but always have a business card at the ready. Talk to people with enthusiasm and excitement. You and your teaching are the best forms of advertisement. Give great service to your clients. Keep your focus on them and their goals and they'll do the advertising for you!

CHAPTER 7

The Price Is Right

"The acquirement and enjoyment of physical well-being, mental calm, and spiritual peace are priceless to their possessors...(and) it is only through controlology that this unique trinity of a balanced body, mind, and spirit can ever be attained."

~ Joseph Pilates

WHETHER you work out of your home, travel to your client's homes or rent space at a studio, if you have chosen to be an independent contractor, the dollar signs are now in your hands. This chapter addresses the decisions involved with the financial value of sessions, client packages, taxes and the true cost of a client. If you decide to work on payroll for a fitness club, studio or office many of these decisions are left to the business owners but knowing your worth is crucial as "How much?" will likely be asked by every client you meet, regardless of the venue.

SO..."How much?" If you are an independent contractor, your answer depends on several factors: location, rent or other business expenses, teaching experience/ niche and monetary needs. Before you start scheduling clients, you will want to figure these things out. Looking at the rates of other local teachers might be helpful for comparing rates, but just copying them without crunching your numbers is pointless. The rates other teachers charge for private sessions are based on what they need to profit to successfully run their business. If you're teaching in your home, or at a client's home, your rates might be vastly different. Food for thought:

- Teaching in your own home, you don't have to pay rent to a studio owner but you have different expenses like additional insurance coverage and equipment maintenance.

- If you're traveling to client's homes, you won't be paying rent to a studio, but you will be doing more driving, car maintenance and possibly paying costs for additional props.

- If you are renting space from someone how much will the rent per session or per specific period be?

- How much money in taxes will you need to pay?

- Time spent emailing, making phone calls, scheduling and doing yourself promotion and marketing outreach is all valuable.

- Your teaching hours do not start and end with a Pilates session. Clients with specific fitness needs or injuries will require you to spend time doing research or possibly starting continuing education for specialized training techniques.

- You may need to purchase special props for a client.

- Parking? Is there free parking for you or will you need to pay for parking. Not easy to move your car every couple hours!

- Coffee, tea, snacks?

- Studio shoes, uniform?

- Cell phone, internet, PayPal

FIRST **you need to determine your single session price.** Give this decision a lot of thought! Charge too much and you might not fill your schedule, charge too little and after paying all your teaching expenses you might be left with nothing to show for your time and efforts. It is common to offer packages for multiple sessions, usually 3 or 5 and 10. Package prices should lower the price of each session by a few dollars. Offering packages means your client will be committed to you and Pilates for a certain number of sessions. Packages are useful for both the instructor and the client because, as you may have experienced yourself, Pilates isn't mastered in one, two or even 5 sessions. Even Joseph said "in 10 sessions you'll feel different, 20 sessions you'll look different, 30 sessions you'll have a whole new body. If you take 3-4x a week." When a client commits to a 10 session package, that gives the instructor 10 sessions to really translate the exercise into the experience of Pilates as Joseph Pilates intended.

Once you've set your rates stick to them. You want to have the same rates for all of your clients. Having clients paying different rates can get confusing for you, and should a client find out they are paying more than their friend can be detrimental to your business. Remember, word of mouth advertising is one of the biggest tools for gaining clients, and you might not even know that your clients know each other. So, as much as you might like a client and want to give them a little break on a package it's best to keep it all the same. Part of being a professional is running your business professionally. Clients will respect that you have financial integrity even if they hint about wanting a "special" discount.

Set your rates and create a rate card (See additional material for example). Making a rate card is nice because it's easy to email, post signage or hand in person to a potential client. If you're gun shy talking about money it's much easier to say "here are my rates" and hand them a card. The rate card should also have a cancellation policy on it as well.

If you plan on teaching duets, semi privates or classes you will have more rates to create. If you have packages for privates it's easy and consistent to have packages for duets/semis. While you'll command a higher hourly fee for these multi-person session, your studio rent may be higher for multi-client sessions. Coordinating session times can be tricky, but duets and semis can be great options for clients who are able to be flexible, and fun and lucrative for you as the instructor. Teaching them might mean a little extra work on your part but the group energy is exciting to work with! Sometimes, it is helpful for business building to teach duets to clients that have friends or family members interested in Pilates, and they can do the schedule haggling amongst themselves. If you have a client who is hesitant about the expense of a single session, you can upsell the idea of doing Pilates with a friend or family member and getting a reduced duet rate.

The longer it takes a client to use their package, the more time between "paydays." To this end, think about assigning an expiration date when selling packages. Also, if a client has a last minute cancellation, you will already have the payment for that session and can bill accordingly. That package then becomes security for payment. Packages will provide you a little less money than an individual session fee, but most teachers feel packages are helpful for building business.

Most teachers do not like the fee conversation but keep in mind you are teaching a session in exchange for a payment. Whether this is a part-time or full-time teaching job you are working and should be compensated for your time. Knowing what your sessions are worth is key to your success as a teacher. Set rates reflecting the value of your sessions, and focus on your clients getting value out of every session.

There are several ways of discussing rates with a potential client. It will depend on how the client finds you. For example, if you are standing in line at a coffee shop doing your "Elevator speech" they might ask you right there, "How much do you charge?" Just tell them. Be clear and confident. If you say it as if you believe it's too expensive, they will pick up on your energy. **Do not waver when discussing prices.** Take special caution in a place where you are not the owner and where the rates have been determined by someone else. Do not get into an *"us vs. them."* Suggesting disapproval of the studio's rates and policies will not help you to gain clients. **Practice saying your rates, package offers and financial policies on a friend or family member until you can speak about money clearly and confidently.** If a person contacts you through your website or other social media you should respond back quickly by attaching your rate card, or you can choose to have your prices clearly displayed on your website.

Let clients know ahead of time what forms of payment you accept. The clearer and organized you are the simpler the fee conversation can go. If you have an iPad or smartphone, there are several options for taking client credit cards. They have different fees attached so check them all out before deciding. Square.com is a popular way to accept credit cards. With a simple attachment and swipe of a credit card, you will receive payment into your account in 1-3 days. It has no monthly costs, simply charges you a 2.75% transaction fee.

THERE will be clients that will always push for a discount or maybe even go through a hardship that could make financially continuing Pilates difficult. As an instructor you can become friendly or close with your clients, and you might begin to feel guilty or tempted to help them out. Remind yourself that it's better in the long run if your rates are the same for everyone. You still have to pay your bills and run your business, and if every time a client needed a discount gave in, when will it end? Some clients might go through hardships and rearrange their budgets to keep Pilates a priority, and would never ask for a discount. It's fair for all involved if you don't let your emotions get involved with your session rates. There is always the worry that if you don't give in to the discount request, you'll lose them as a client. But lose a client who is always looking for a discount, you gain an opening in your schedule for a more consistent client. If you lose a client for financial reasons, know that it is only your job to assist them reaching their fitness goals, and when they can afford to book time with you again, they will return.

If you have interest in doing a discount price package with a company like Groupon, Living Social, Gilt City or Goldstar, make sure to do your research. It might be good for advertising, but not for your bottom line. If you are just looking to increase your public profile and get some interest from outside your personal circle--great. But be prepared for a lot of traffic that might not pay much either in profit or permanent clients. Because these kinds of promotions are so prevalent right now in social media, a lot of people gym-hop, or just go from package deal to package deal, without settling in to one teacher or one studio. If you are opening your own stu-dio, it might be great just to increase awareness about your local business, but if you have a decent schedule, or work for a studio, gym, or office just keep doing what you are doing. If the studio you work for decides to offer an online special, understand that you may have some new clients scheduled who have no experience with or knowledge of Pilates, and it is your job to give the best session you can, and hopefully the 3 or 5 sessions will be enough to convince the client to pull out their check-book and commit to the real rates. You can always make up a 50% postcard for all your clients to give to a friend, and give them a 50% off for every referral they bring in. Do what is comfortable, and never feel like you have to discount or decrease your rate for anyone. Your clients don't expect less of your teaching value, so don't trade your worth for a quick "special of the day".

MONEY! Money! Money! Now that you've made some, where does it all go? A few pointers, if you choose to rent space in a studio:

- Make sure you are clear about exactly when your rental fees are due.

- Make a copy of your session log, and attach it to the rent check. For example, a duet session might require you to pay $32 in rent, and a private $18, so make sure you have detailed notes that can back up your financial statements.

- Always pay your rent with a check, if there is ever a discrepancy you can always contact your bank.

- Consider opening up a separate checking account for depositing client's checks and paying your business expenses. When this "business" account money is separate from a personal checking account, it is easier to track your expenses and you can "pay" yourself a salary. Check with the bank you currently use and see what sort of business accounts they offer.

IF you are working for a doctor's office, fitness facility or health club you will most likely be on payroll. Each business will have a payroll schedule and you should always keep track of your own client sessions, and any other shared clients or classes you may substitute teach. Even if the studio has an online schedule software program, it's a good idea to keep your own detailed log so you know what to financially expect for your work, and so you can plan ahead in your own life for personal expenses, etc.

TAXES are no fun, but no matter how you earn a living, you have to report your income. There are wonderful accountants out there, who can help you understand everything you need to know, as tax laws change often, and may be different in every state. Always consult a professional when dealing with a new business. You may have business license fees, city business tax and estimated quarterly tax payments. But business owner or not, keep every "business" receipt. You may designate a specific credit card for business expenses, and can use the statement to keep organized. General guidelines:

- When you are an employee on a payroll, the company will automatically take out taxes on your behalf. Check your pay stub to be sure you are paying into both your state and federal taxes so you're not presented with a big surprise come April 15th.

- If you are considered an independent contractor, and no taxes are being withheld, find out if you're current on what you owe Uncle Sam before spending that first paycheck.

- If you are going to work as an "independent contractor" you'll need to fill out a W9 form. You may also be asked for a W2, W4, or I9. According to www.ucis.gov an I9 form needs to be filled out by anyone working in the US. You'll need to provide your Social Security number or documents showing you are able to work in the US.

- As an independent contractor you get to deduct your business expenses against your gross income. Your taxes would include what is called a Schedule C. This is where you would itemize your expenses. Since the IRS audits Schedule C's, you will need to find an organization system that works for you. Records of your mileage and income will need to be maintained. For example, if you're deducting auto expenses you must record a daily mileage. And know the rules and boundaries of claiming expenses. The miles to and from the studio do not count, they are considered "commuter miles." Those Lululemon tights might be all you wear for Pilates, but because you can also wear them outside of work they do not qualify as a tax write off, however if you are required to wear a "uniform", like all black clothing, or you have specific teaching wear that you don't use elsewhere, that could be a deductible expense. You might purchase a box set of Pilates DVD's to learn some new exercises, this is a "business expense," but your cable is not. **Keep every receipt, and everything organized.**

- Some people who are self-employed choose to pay estimated taxes quarterly. This option is helpful in breaking up any taxes you have to pay. Taxable income can range from 0% to 45%. Check with your accountant to find out what percentage you can expect to pay. Which leads to the important question to ask yourself. Do you know how to prepare your taxes, now that you are self-employed? If not it's best to hire someone. While it's an expense, it saves you time, frustration, confusion, stress and maybe even money!

WHEN figuring out your teaching costs and expenses, it is important to consider the entire cost of keeping a client, and the biggest fee is the value of your time. It is necessary to consider how to meet your client's needs, while figuring out the costs of running a business. It might seem like a lot of work to get started, but it will pay off in the end.

> Katherine Slay, teacher of 10 years: "At the core of this crazy vocation, for me, is the relationships. When I first started teaching, there was a struggle of me finding my own voice, trying to sell a lifestyle which I believe in, and trying to make a living. It's a process. "

CHAPTER 8

Clients and Realities

"In 10 sessions you will feel the difference, in 20 sessions you will see the difference, and in 30 you will have a whole new body."

~ Joseph Pilates

THESE days it's hard to buy anything or go anywhere without encountering rules and policies. They are the boundaries that create the infrastructure of modern-day business. You need to be upfront and consistent with any policies you create. If employed by a studio or office, make sure you understand and enforce any policies or rules they have put in place. The client should be aware of these policies before putting even a toe on a piece of equipment. Any policies or rules can be included on your rate card, should be posted in your work environment and you can also be incorporated into reminders on voicemails/emails when confirming appointments. When a new client signs their release liability, have them sign their acknowledgement underneath a "rules/policies" section as well.

THE Rules:

- Cancellation policies are common in a service industry. Most doctor's offices, fitness clubs or private exercise studios will have one in place. Typically a private session can be cancelled 24 hour prior to the appointment. If the client does "late cancel," giving less than 24 hours notice, they might be charged the full rate of the session. For a group class of 5 or more, some studios allow cancellations up to an hour prior to a class, but that is usually because they have an online automatic waitlist system. Teaching duets and semi-privates might require a stricter cancellation policy, as the rate changes with the size of the session. A 48 hour cancellation policy might seem too rigid to enforce, but you need to think of everyone in the session, not just the client who needs to reschedule.   If you are creating your own cancellation policy, you can decide how strict you want to be.

- There can also be a cancellation policy for instructors. If you are sick and need to call out at the last minute, the client may receive a free session, or be given a substitute teacher and you might risk losing that client. Make sure you are responsible when it comes to any rescheduling you might need to do, and always communicate with your clients. Don't allow your absence to be a surprise, and don't let the studio receptionist be the messenger of your bad news.

- Rules on tardiness are suggested as well, not just because of time management. If a client joins a class 15 minutes late, they might not get a good warm up and can injure themselves by jumping right into the workout. Private clients are different, and sometimes the "late" policy can be tricky to enforce. Depending on where you live or teach, there can be a multitude of reasons a client is late. It's important to have a clear and consistent policy. If the client is late then they lose their own session time. The more consistent you are, the less stress you will have enforcing this policy. If a client is late, they don't get to go 5 minutes longer, even if there is no one scheduled after them. Always check with your employer's policy on handling late clients. **If you are in business for yourself, remember your time is money, and safety comes first.**

- How long does a client have to use their purchased package sessions? Check with those in charge before you start selling packages, so you are clear with the rules of the purchase. If self-employed, you might want to consider how long you'll want to keep track of a package. Six months? A year? Forever? The choice is yours. An expiration policy keeps clients committed to their practice and keeps them on a schedule. It can also be a smarter financial decision for you to create an expiration date with goal that clients will use their sessions up and buy again. **Have clients sign in for their session so they can see exactly where they are in their package sessions and begin to plan for their next purchase when appropriate.**

SOMEONE will always ask to bend the rules. If you work for a studio, office, or gym, let the management handle it. If it is your own client, that you are renting space for, it is up to you. *But be careful.* **Pay attention to the habits of the clients, a perpetual latecomer is**

not someone that should get an extra 5 minutes of your time. If a client has an emergency, and they have never asked for any rule-bending before, decide if it's ok to let a late-cancel slide. Always articulate that you both acknowledge the rule-bending, and this is a one-time only exception. This is all about your comfort level, you don't need to change or bend your rules and policies for anyone! Be fair, to yourself and to your clients. Don't be afraid to enforce your policies. Chances are if clients feel the sting of a late cancel, they won't do it again and if Pilates stays at the top of their priority list, they will achieve their fitness goals quickly, and with you to thank.

How often should your clients schedule Pilates for the best possible results? **Joseph Pilates expected at least 3 to 4 times a week.** Most clients would like to do 2 to 3 times a week, but the reality of scheduling and budgets can sometimes bring it down to 1 time a week. A good rule of thumb is a client should do a minimum of 4 sessions in a month. A once-weekly client that is leaving town for 2 weeks should double up before they leave to ensure they have their 4 sessions. Obviously clients that are more frequent and consistent will see the best results. You have two options when scheduling clients, you can proactively schedule them or you can let them decide when to schedule themselves. Most clients need you to be proactive in keeping them on track. Having "standing" sessions that are prescheduled will help everyone to plan ahead and keep Pilates as a priority.

Clients take vacations, have meetings and encounter different events that will require you to occasionally move a session. Instead of a straight cancel, always try to reschedule. You don't want to lose the session, not just for financial reasons, but also so your client feels the momentum of a consistent Pilates practice.

There are those clients who will be unable to reschedule; if they miss a week, they might go two weeks or more between sessions. As an instructor, this is a difficult scenario. Of course there is the understanding that life is busy, but for a client, missing that much time in between sessions might cause them to doubt the results of the practice. This is a common way to lose a client; lack of results, which might be due to circumstances out of your control.

If a client is having a hard time keeping their appointments, offer them alternative times, and be honest with them about the importance of finding an hour or two in their week that can be devoted to them, their health and fitness, and having an outlet to develop balance and focus can be beneficial in the rest of their life.

OTHER reasons for losing a client and what to do:

- Income can ebb and flow and everyone experiences the pinch of an unexpected expense. If your client purchases packages, they will save a few dollars, and if they can only schedule week-to-week, help them understand the financial priority of the

Pilates session, by reinforcing the idea that health is priceless. Give them sessions that exceed their monetary value. If a client is looking and feeling their best, they are more likely to skip a few lattes to get in an extra Pilates session. If a client takes a break for financial reasons, give them a few weeks or a month, and then contact them to say hello and check in. Maybe you have a possible duet partner or new group class that might work for them? Most clients will appreciate that you thought of them and are trying to accommodate their situation.

- If a client has taken a break due to health issues checking in from time to time just see how they're doing is appropriate. As an instructor, you get close to your clients and checking in on their recovery is normal. Of course in any situation, you don't want to overdo it with your "check-ins." Every client is unique, feel them out. If the client says they need 6 weeks off to recover, check in after a week or so just to see how they're doing. Then a week or so before their expected return check in to confirm their recovery is on track to confirm the expected date is still on.

- A client you lose due to location change doesn't mean the relationship is over. They might have friends or family still in your area who might want to take over their time slot. Keep in touch through email or a nice card; if they come back to visit, maybe they will want to fit in a session.

YOU might be the one taking a break or long vacation. The sooner you communicate your scheduling changes to your clients, you will have time to book them some extra sessions before you leave. If you notice a particularly empty weekend on your books, maybe that should be your time to plan a quick getaway. The goal is to disrupt your clients sessions and schedules as little as possible, regardless of your personal plans.

Connecting with your clients is an important part of the teacher client relationship. Conversations about weekend plans or work projects will come up. These conversations can be helpful for you with scheduling, and keep them on track with their sessions. But, it's easy for these conversations to become personal, and sometimes take precedent over the exercise. It's important to stay on task and keep Pilates as your focus. Keep in mind that while the client might be comfortable sharing or even "oversharing" it doesn't give you an invitation to turn their Pilates session into your therapy sessions. Always keep your professional boundaries during session time. You may develop close relationship with clients, especially after years of session. They still don't need to know if you are struggling financially, fighting with your boyfriend or even just having a bad day. The session is about them. Beware of the nosy client who wants to talk about what's going on in your life or want to gossip about your other clients. Keep the session on target, do your best to be friendly and professional without divulging more about yourself than you need to and keep your other's clients progress, personal information and schedules confidential. The more you are able to keep the focus on Pilates, the less they will have the opportunity to engage you in gossip.

Perhaps the teachers that work alongside you want to ask personal questions about you and/or your clients, or be inappropriately chatty or nosy. Be careful what you say and where you say it. Excuse yourself from the conversation or just change the subject. Teaching your clients the session they're paying for is top priority, and you never know who might be friends or family with whom; if you keep your lips zipped, your clients can always feel safe.

There will always be clients who are too chatty, or maybe cross the personal line with comments here and there. Those verbal violators are usually easily handled with boundaries. It's the touchy-feely and possible sexual advances that need to be addressed directly and swiftly. Though never expected, and rarely experienced, when you are up close and personal with someone else's body, you need to be prepared. When you are teaching, whether it is a female or male client, your touch should be appropriate quick and concise, and strictly for emphasis in an exercise. Always ask if you can before you lay hands on your client. You may teach a session where the client inappropriately touches you. Don't ignore this. If you let it happen once, it may happen again and the inappropriate behavior can escalate. You are the instructor, you control the session. Don't let a clients misguided intentions, whether verbal or physical, take over the session. **If you have been clear and professional yet you still feel unsafe or uncomfortable teaching someone it is more than appropriate to end your teacher-client relationship.** If you have a boss or office manager, talk with them and follow their protocol. If you work for yourself, return the client's money for any unused sessions. You can either suggest another teacher that is willing to take them on, or just simply thank them and say in front of a witness that you can no longer teach them.

Things can get tricky is when your friends and family start taking sessions. They might feel they should have a friends and family discount. It's ultimately up to you how you decide to handle it. It's easier on you and places a higher importance on the session if you try to treat them as you would any other client. While they are taking a session teach them with professionalism as you would any other client. The late cancellation policy and tardiness policies should still apply. Just because they are a friend of yours doesn't mean they don't have to respect your business policies. If you feel at some point that it would be better for all involved if they switch to a different instructor, explain to them why it's better for the personal relationship if they work with someone else. Set up their first session, follow up and make sure all involved are happy and situated. The less you avoid the topic and the sooner you handle it, the better for everyone.

Inevitably, after months or years of sessions, clients naturally become friends but you should never lose sight of the business relationship that exists. They are coming to you for a service, paying for a service and you are providing that service. You may be invited to their weddings, yard sales, baby showers, parties etc. The decision is yours whether you decide to go. Their sessions, rates, time etc should stay consistent with your other clients. It will be easy to maintain the business relationship as long as you're consistent.

CHAPTER 9

Popular Knowledge

"Controlology is not a fatiguing system of dull, boring, abhorred exercises repeated daily 'ad nauseum'."

~ *Joseph Pilates*

YOUR apprenticeship program will prepare you to teach a substantial amount of Pilates exercises to the majority of people. However, it's impossible to learn every exercise in a short period of time. How to tailor the exercises for special groups of clients is usually discovered through experience and continuing education. There is a lot of research and discussion about how Pilates can help specific groups of people like expectant mothers or senior citizens. If you come across a body type or body goal that is unfamiliar to you, investigate it and see where research and continuing education will take you. If you ultimately develop a niche clientele, use that to spin how you market yourself.

Pilates is often recommended in maternity circles. No two bodies or bellies are alike and what works for one pregnant client doesn't always work for another. In your program, you hopefully were given some important do's and dont's for expectant clients. Many people think that pregnancy means changing your workout routine completely. Not necessarily. In the first trimester, most healthy women having "routine" pregnancy can continue the fitness work they were already doing pre-pregnancy. As the pregnancy continues, exercises will be adjusted or eliminated.

Most important is the a-ok from their doctor. Communication between you and your client is also vital; you need to be in constant discussion about what she is feeling and where she is experiencing any intensity or discomfort. As the instructor, be sure to communicate that the sessions will look and feel different than what they are used to doing prior to pregnancy. With careful planning and communication Pilates will be your pregnant client's best fitness regime throughout her entire pregnancy. However, use all resources available; particularly senior instructors make sure you are being safe, safe, safe. When in doubt, leave it out.

Once your expectant client has had her baby, stay in touch with her for when she is ready to return. The average woman has to wait 4-6 weeks after a vaginal delivery before resuming exercise, c-section birth 8-12 weeks. Most important is that she has her doctor's permission to come back to Pilates. Your client will not pick up right where they left off! Be prepared to start back at the beginning. Their mind and muscle memory may be intermediate/advanced but their body can be much like a beginners. They'll need to re-discover their powerhouse and you'll want to watch out for any new asymmetries. Go slow, be patient, and focus on balance, breathing and the mind-body connection.

A surprisingly beneficial relationship is the one between Pilates and golfers! Pilates for golfers has been popular for a few years now, and there are several instructional books and dvd's on the subject. If you have clients that golf, you will find out pretty fast that they would rather be on the course than in the studio, but they will also doing anything to improve their golf game. With enough research and planning Pilates can not only help them swing better and hit the ball farther but also help them feel better after their round of golf! **Someone who originally had little interest in Pilates can become an enthusiast if it'll improve their game and keep them injury free.**

Golfing, like many sports puts stress, strain and causes asymmetries in the body. According to www.ideafit.com, golfers have limited torso flexibility and imbalanced musculature.   As a Pilates instructor, muscular imbalances will be nothing new to you. Focusing on exercises that strengthen the core and the hips as well as opening the chest will be where you start.   However, your job isn't only about keeping them under par. Be sure to take a look at how their shoulders sit while they're doing their Pilates session. While they are there for a better stroke count, you are also there to keep their body balanced. Spot training isn't the style of Pilates, creating length and balance, strength and flexibility through the entire body is your goal, even while you may tailor exercises for your client.

Dancers love Pilates, in fact most people are under the false impression that Pilates is only meant for dancers. While many dancers are blessed with a long lean "dancers" body, this doesn't mean they don't need Pilates for other reasons. Dancers who struggle with turnouts and flexibility will find Pilates to be a key to their success, as the practice aides in flexibility while strengthening their body. Many dancers lack the required core strength, and end up with weak lower backs and weak abdominal muscles. This poor posture leads to poor alignment and poor technique. Often dancers work in a sway back to achieve the ideal turnout. Pilates teaches its practitioners how to use the proper muscle groups. Dancers who use Pilates to learn how to work from their core will gain the strength to stand taller and use the muscles of their body to achieve the lines and turn outs they desire[2].

Keep in mind that your dancer clients can make the exercises "look" amazing. Be sure you are watching for proper alignment and not just end range of flexibility. Keep them in the muscles rather than hanging out in their joints. With dancers, take the Pilates exercises to the full extension and demand perfect alignment. For example, elephant on the reformer is a great exercise for most clients. Stretching the backs of the legs while opening up the back, and requiring the client to stabilize their shoulders is a challenging exercise for everyone. Try having your dancer do elephant with one leg in arabesque--you are getting all the benefits plus the additional practice of balance and hip stability.

Dancers are used to stretching long, and will easily grasp the idea of lengthening through their limbs, but can they focus on the resistance of the exercise? Do a warm up of footwork on the reformer, with the focus being on the control of bringing the carriage in, not just the extension of taking the carriage out. Performing Pilates can look and feel like dance, but the difference is the control and intention of a strong core to initiate all movement, and the mind-body focus of stability through movement. It is key for dancers to improve their strength

2 Elona Sherwood, Yahoo Contributors

while in a controlled movement to protect and prevent against injury. Research the difference between open chain and closed chain movement, and you will see a whole other side of Pilates, which is helpful in working with those already blessed with flexibility and length. **Let local dancers know about your teaching, go to local dancewear shops, studios and performing art stages posting the benefits of Pilates for dancers, with your card attached!**

Pilates may have received early popularity with the dance crowd of New York, but it was created by a man, and a tough-guy at that! While modern men are often skeptical about Pilates, once you get them in a session and teach them the method, they are usually shocked at the intensity of the workout! If you are not a male instructor, get a second opinion either from a master teacher or a male teacher on your plan for springs. You will most likely have to adjust the reformer by blocking out the carriage, and may need specific props to help with tight hip flexors, a common male trait. You may also need to adjust your cuing; teaching **with more direct cues rather than colorful imagery tends to work better for men.**

Just like dancers can wow with hyper-mobility, men can "muscle" through an exercise and your teaching 'eyes' need to be present and precise. As you know, if you're not doing Pilates with the correct start position, and initiating form the proper muscles group, an exercise can be very easy and feel silly or useless to the client.

Jeremy Braithwaite, Pilates client of 2 years, practicing 2-3x a week:
"I had always been under the impression that Pilates was for women only and was skeptical of the benefits it would have for me personally. How wrong I was!"

Being able to articulate the benefits of Pilates for men will help fill your schedule with a great balance of men and women or maybe you become the go-to Pilates teacher just for men! Pilates is a great form of cross training for men who enjoy weight lifting, as they are usually concentrating on only one muscle group at a time.   They may have a harder time with flexibility, but assure them that is not the most important element of a great Pilates workout.   **Make sure to give the dress code to a new male client to avoid any awkward situations.**
The latest Olympic Games brought increased attention to Pilates as an essential part of athletic training. Misty May Treanor, Natalie Coughlin and Lolo Jones have all expressed their love of Pilates and incorporate Pilates exercises in their training. Pilates isn't just a workout for athletes, but also a way of keeping symmetry in their bodies. Training for their individual sports can leave an athlete over developed in some areas, and weaker in others. Pilates brings a balance to their physical body as well as a way for them to train their brain in mind-body awareness, and mindful movements. This kind of training helps to prevent

injuries and assists in developing heightened focus and goal attainment.

From www.powerpilates.com website, "RW McQuarters, cornerback for the NY Giants, considers Pilates as crucial to his pro athlete performance and career. McQuarters trains in Rutherford, NJ with instructor Jody Domerstad. PilatesStyle Magazine reports that McQuarters was simply looking for a way to be flexible since the team stretching he did on the field did not seem like enough.

Interestingly, his previous team, the Chicago Bears, made yoga mandatory for the team as so many players suffered from pulled muscles. What is amazing is that he has not had a muscle injury since he began doing Pilates one year ago. He is quoted as saying "Using the machine to hep you hold certain positions take you deeper into the stretch". McQuarters feels that even fifteen minutes can help to release the lactic acid in his body and soreness. He finds himself at the Pilates studio in NJ at least three nights a week after a full day of practice. He continues to do some yoga, but he personally feels that Pilates gives him better results. McQuarters admits his toughest muscles to stretch are those tight hamstrings.

Some days he feels like leaving, but he works through the pain and always ends up feeling better. Pilates has helped him stay off the training table and on the field playing. He also reports sleeping better, feeling looser, and feeling more length in his muscles. Having a Superbowl ring on his finger will hopefully keep him motivated to continue his Pilates training and inspire others to start Pilates, too!"

WHEN training an athlete it's important to keep in mind what they are already practicing, and make sure you are focusing on balancing the body. A sprinter wouldn't need as much leg strengthening, as they would need leg stretching and upper body strengthening. It's also important to keep your job is to keep them on the road to health and balance. You are not a doctor or a coach! You may or may not have a background and diploma as a physical therapist or personal fitness trainer, so always remember, when in doubt leave it out!

Pilates is also a perfect fit for older clients who need extra attention to balance work, without a lot of shock or stress to the bones. Check out the local country clubs for bridge tournaments, book clubs or senior-specific activities, and leave information on Pilates, specific to the benefits on a senior body. Elderly clients will require modifications and/or props to help them get in and out of exercises but they can do more than one would think they could. Like pregnant clients, there are guidelines to follow in the beginning, but since every person is different and each client has different aches and pains don't just throw away exercises without attempting a variation.

As clients age, they begin to struggle with balance. Getting creative to challenge and strengthen their balance will keep them from falling and potentially hurting themselves. Spine flexibility and strength is also a focus for elderly clients. The core conditioning of Pilates keeps them standing taller and the exercises that require twisting and side bending, while more challenging, are exactly what they need to have a strong healthy spine. As Joseph said "you're only as old as your spine is young," Your elderly clients will start with you and get "younger" as they continue. The American Association of Retired Persons agrees that Pilates' emphasis on stretching and strengthening core muscles, "wards of the effects of aging!" Pilates is also great for elderly clients because it's low impact on their joints, unlike many other forms of fitness. **Additionally, Pilates provides elderly clients mental exercise to stay sharp, in control and coordinated!** If anyone says they're too old for Pilates, shout it from the rooftops that Joe practiced until he was in his 80's!

Often instructors find themselves with a specific clientele because of their own Pilates experience. If you're an ex-athlete, relating your Pilates experience to potential clients helps them connect to you and your teaching. If you decide to specialize in any of these listed populations, marketing yourself within those groups is a great way to set yourself apart from the average instructor. It also narrows down where you advertise the continuing education you seek and puts you in a path to become an expert in that field. Putting yourself in a specialized niche might seem limiting, but if you're getting your client results, their teammates, friends or family will come too!

CHAPTER 10

How To Have A Life

"A few well designed movements, properly performed in a balanced sequence, are worth hours of doing sloppy calisthenics or forced contortion."

~ *Joseph Pilates*

IN the beginning of your teaching career, your focus is on teaching as much as possible. You'll teach any time of day or night just to fill up your schedule. But as you're working to fill your calendar, where do "you" fit in? It is common at the start of any new career or endeavor, to put the work first and yourself second. Even though you might not be a 9-to-5er, in a traditional office setting, you will still need to create a work schedule that leaves time for you. You need time for your own practice, appointments, a day off, whatever. To stay inspired and fresh for your clients, you need time away from teaching. Map out your schedule, organize as best you can, and protect your personal time like a precious gem, because your time is valuable.

Begin with your calendar, whether it's on your phone or hanging on your wall. The first thing to figure out is your "actual" availability. Whatever is going on in your life, block out the hours you already know are not available for teaching. Also block out one day off. **Make sure you have one day just for yourself and protect it!** Then determine when you want to teach. There are hours that tend to be more popular than others. Many clients book sessions before work, after work or on Saturday and Sunday mornings. A lot of clients are also able to book session during the middle of the day, perhaps if they work at night, if they have school-age children or if they can get to the gym on their lunch break. Remember, **a good Pilates instructor can fill any schedule they desire to work with thoughtful planning.**

If you are a night owl, perhaps you want to focus on booking afternoon and evening sessions. If you are an early bird, maybe your 6am bookings will be full every weekday. When are you at your best? If you are some-one who cannot wake up in the morning, and feel grumpy until noon, do not spend your energy on trying to turn yourself into a 5am instructor. To give your clients the best level of service, you must make sure your sched-ule will serve you both. Your goal is to see each client at least twice a week, if their finances and your mutual schedule allows. A Monday person will most likely want a Wednesday or Friday. **It's useful to be a available at**

the same time every other day. Make sure you offer optional days when booking a repeat session, so clients know sessions are available on multiple days at their desired time.

The next question to help determine your schedule is how many hours a day can you teach? You might be used to an 8 or 9 hour day, and think that you can keep up with those hours, but teaching private sessions and clients is not like a regular job, even if you keep a traditional schedule. When you're teaching, you are keeping tremendous focus, you are doing a lot of talking, intense observation, standing, possibly demonstrating, and there is no "down" moment in your hour. Your brain, your mouth and your body need breaks to recharge. You need time for snacks, lunch, a walk in the fresh air. You might be comfortable doing a 4 hour stint in the morning, getting a few hours break, and doing another 4 hour block in the evening. You might cap at 6 clients in a day. Hopefully, while completing your apprentice hours you got a feel for your own teaching stamina. You want to be the best teacher possible, and if you are great for 5 sessions and "good" during the 6th, definitely weigh whether or not you want to add a 7th.

Be thoughtful about leaving our schedule totally open. You might have 4 private sessions booked on a Tuesday, but if they are at 6am, 1130am, 5pm and 8pm, is that the best way to book your day? It's up to you if you want that long of a day, or maybe that's perfect so you can do errands or studying in between. Perhaps those will be your "marketing" hours where you focus on your social media, or reaching out to prospective clients, or write a blog. Or you might have to schedule your day spaced apart because you are traveling to multiple teaching locations. Whatever the case, be realistic about time spent commuting, and time you may need during the business day to returns phone calls and emails. An hour not spent teaching is not necessarily an hour wasted, it gives you the power and opportunity to make that hour work for you. But also be realistic about how much downtime is too much; downtime can easily become wasted time.

Eventually, you will come to a place where you just have to "let go" letting go of a difficult client, or letting go of pushing yourself through one extra session. If you have a client that is very difficult to schedule around your availability, help them find another instructor. **If a client only wants to work with you, they need to do the rearranging, not you.** You won't always be able to please every client or teach every person that wants to be your student. It can be stressful in the beginning to say "no" to a client, fear of losing potential income can make you run at them with open arms and an open schedule. But 'when one door closes, another door opens!' Perhaps the client who is always doing late cancels, or can only come a time you can't offer, has to go with another instructor. That only frees you up to find a client who wants to do Pilates three times a week and never misses! Had the other client not left your schedule you might not have had space for this new, stable client. The fear of losing a client can make you want to bend over backwards for them, but what about you?

If you are firm about your "unavailable" hours, which will hopefully motivate clients to keep their appointments, and prevent cancellations. There will be times when a good client wants a session on your usual day off.   It's up to you to decide if you want to take that session. When you're not teaching you're not earning an income, however, if you make an exception this time, will you be firm enough to protect your "me" time, next time? Preserving your day off and letting your clients know you are unavailable on that day, or maybe even just 'that afternoon,' will help them plan their schedule accordingly. If something comes up that will affect their scheduled session, and switching it might mean missing a week of Pilates altogether, hopefully they will protect their session time better in the future. One missed session and they'll realize that keeping their Pilates hour is priority! If you decide to teach on your regularly scheduled day off, verbally acknowledge to the client that this is a special treat and not a regular option.

Changing your schedule to accommodate clients will affect your teaching and your personal life. Eventually you will resent your own clients, or tire from constantly changing your schedule and you might feel drained, uninspired and unappreciated. You don't want to bring that kind of energy to all of your clients, when it's just a few that are causing problems. **Try to stick to your own**

scheduling boundaries. You must preserve yourself to be at your best for your steady clientele, otherwise there is no Pilates business for you. Boundaries and planning will keep your schedule full and under your control.

Many instructors become certified because they simply just love Pilates and what it does for their own body. When you're an apprentice you rarely have to worry about fitting in your own practice, you are required to be doing hours of Pilates every week. Once you are an instructor, it is easy to put off your own sessions in favor of a paying client. You might do a little self-practice in between sessions, but when is the last time you took a session from another instructor? You should be aiming for 2 to 3 sessions a week, just like you would advise your clientele. Think about how great you felt after your last session. Think about how great your clients feel.

"Keep taking your own session!! Every session I take as a client, I learn so many things to take and teach to my own clients. Practice what you preach, and do Pilates as much as you recommend it for your clients." Jeni Del Pozo, teacher of 7 months

SELF-PRACTICE is necessary to inform you as an instructor and taking Pilates from a more experienced teacher that inspires you will help you grow and progress in your own practice. If you can commit to an hour a week with a senior teacher, you are giving yourself an hour to perfect an exercise, to ask questions or just to quiet your mind and enjoy your practice. You should never stop learning and refining your Pilates. Keeping your sessions a priority will keep you from feeling like you're always giving and not receiving. If finances are an issue think about trading teaching hours with a fellow teacher, or taking a duet or semi. Some training studios offer "pro" classes specifically for teachers and trainers. The important thing is taking a session from another instructor to keep your cues fresh, your body strong and your Pilates infused with joy. **If you're not inspired, your clients can tell.**

As discussed earlier, continuing education is part of the teacher's life. As you deepen your practice and your teaching experience increases, you might have questions about equipment or exercises, or have heard about a particular instructor you'd like to learn from. Workshops are a great way to deepen your knowledge and progress your teaching. Many teachers and Pilates Elders travel around bringing their latest workshops to different studios. Do a simple Internet search on instructors you wish to learn from, or Pilates topics you want to get more info on, you can locate workshops in your area or around the country and world! Making a weekend vacation out of it might be worth it if it's something you're really interested in! Workshops usually give you continuing education credit. Check with your certification program to see if a particular workshop qualifies, or if you are certified by Pilates Method Alliance, the PMA site has a list of upcoming approved workshops. If you are a classical teacher, and you want to spend a day exploring contemporary, try and get credit for it. Going to workshops is a great way to meet other instructors and increase your Pilates network. It's nice to have people to call, or email, to help you feel a part of the international Pilates community. It's nice to have a forum to gather with other instructors, ask questions of each other, and explore different styles and ideas.

Conferences are also great places to get continuing education credit. Many certifying programs have weekend or even week long conferences that allow you to get up to two year's worth of continuing education credits. These conferences offer workshops designed by the "host" sponsor. A Gratz conference will offer classical workshops; a Balanced Body conference might showcase new equipment and props. If you attend a PMA or IDEA conference, there will be a variety of teaching styles to observe or experience, all under one roof. Teachers can design a workshop, and submit to the conference host. All conferences offer multiple workshops and continuing education credits, so if it is too difficult to take a single workshop here and there throughout the year, you can get it all done in a weekend, and have a great time too! There are Pilates conventions that draw a huge attendance and you can network with instructors from all over the country, and international Pilates instructors too. It can be expensive to do a weekend away with conference fees, but it might make more sense for your time and money to get the most bang for your buck, and receive the most CE credit for your efforts.

Spending time refining and growing your Pilates practice is necessary but it's not the only exercise you need to do. As you learn to teach Pilates and after you're certified, taking other kinds of fitness classes will increase your knowledge about bodies, health and even inspire new cues to use with your clients. Joseph Pilates gained his knowledge from nature, yoga, boxing, acrobatics and more. Taking Pilates-esque classes like a barre classes, dance and ab classes are fun to do, and are great for meeting potential clients. **It's also important to see what other kinds of fitness moves are appealing to the general public.** You can see how so many modern movements are based on Pilates fundamentals and how they differ. Feel the difference in a basic ab class when you keep your core as tight as when you are doing your hundred. In a body sculpting class, you might find yourself in plank position with a light weight in one hand lifting it up and down. This is using similar muscular contraction as a one-armed push up on the Wunda chair. The next time you have a client struggling with that exercise, you'll have another modification to try.

Staying current on other forms of Pilates like Piloxing®, SPX™ or PilatesPlus© classes offer pilates-style exercises with a twist. You should experience anything being touted as «Pilates» based, so the next time a client asks your thoughts, there is personal experience behind your answer, not just an opinion.

If you have a client who loves yoga, take a yoga class, and learn the difference between «downward facing dog» in yoga and «elephant» in Pilates. It may look similar, but is it? Maybe you train a marathon runner. You don›t need to run a marathon to connect with them but doing some research on common running injuries can help you protect their body. You already know how amazing Pilates is for every person that tries it, but being able to relate to them in language they know makes it easier to connect as a teacher, and as a Pilates enthusiast.

Kathleen Mangan, teacher of 5 years:

"There are many methods of fitness, and you ought to be open to them all, even if all you truly want to teach is Pilates. You have to have a legitimate frame of reference to speak the language that most resonates with your clients, as often they have a very different physical background than I do."

THE more information you have on how Pilates can help your client be more successful in another fitness arena, the better you'll be able to "sell" pilates to a skeptic. There are clients who don't like Pilates but they love to golf. Without Pilates, a frequent golfer can experience asymmetry, tight muscles, painful back injuries, and loss of flexibility. Being able to verbalize the athletic effectiveness of Pilates in their favorite sports or hobbies can mean winning over the ones who'd rather be doing something else.

Don't be afraid of your client announcing they are trying something new. It doesn't have to be a Pilates versus... It can be a Pilates and....! So, keep your mind, your eyes and ears open for new ways to keep your clients and potential clients into new exercises and progressing in fitness. They'll love you for it, thank you for it and keep coming back!

With all the teaching, classes, and workshops it's easy to think you'll be working 24-7! But, as available as you might want to be, it's so important to have at least one day off. Any day is fine--Just pick one and protect it. You know you have it and can plan your life around it. Over teaching is like over training, the body needs a break. So, as you design your schedule if you haven't already picked a day off...go back! Get a permanent marking pen and schedule a no teaching day. You'll be glad to have it!

CHAPTER 11

Your Transition

"To achieve the highest accomplishments within the scope of our capabilities in all walks of life we must constantly strive to acquire strong, healthy bodies and develop our minds to the limits of our ability."

~ Joseph Pilates

MOST likely you were working part time/full time while going through your Pilates apprentice program. Now that you are about to step out into the world of teaching Pilates, you might be wondering when you can leave that other job or even if you should leave your other job. For a part time Pilates instructor, working around the other jobs schedule will be much like going to your apprenticeship. You are already used to the dual schedule and it won't take much reorganizing to keep it. If teaching Pilates full time is your goal, but you're already working full time and financially cannot afford the transition, take your time. Lay your foundation. Get business cards, insurance, research your teaching locations and start spreading the word about your career plans. Get an idea of when are busy teaching times, common vacation times and when you can have some 'you' time. All these things will help set the stage for your next step! Keep the studio hours you had kept as an apprentice, and start putting clients in those time slots. Once those hours are full, and you are ready to add more hours to your teaching schedule let your other job go organically.

The safety job can usually go, once you have the "who, where, and when" set and the available hours you have are already full. As you begin to make your transition, start telling your existing clients that you are opening up your schedule for new people. Let them start the marketing for you! Tweet about it, Facebook about it, ask people to "like," "share," and retweet you, so as many people as possible are getting the information about your teaching updates.   When you are giving your elevator speech, update it to "next week I am adding Mondays and Wednesday mornings!" That tells a prospective client you're in such demand you have to add two more days to get everyone in! Begin selling and filling spots for the new schedule beforehand. This way you won't even have a period of feeling like you are a part time teacher. You'll be coming from your safety job into the full and welcoming schedule of a full time teacher!

> Keep an eye on the calendar. June, July, and August are traveling and family vacation months, summers can be lean.   Leave that safety job in May, and you may get nervous or feel the need to run back!

THE ebbs and flows of income during the summer and holidays are unique those in commission based work, but the flexibility and inspiration that come from teaching help to give a balance. Unlike the safety job, each teaching week's paycheck will vary depending on client's vacations, illnesses or holidays. Planning for a financial rainy day will keep you calm, cool and in the teaching zone.

- Focusing on getting your schedule filled with consistent clients will help you plan your paydays.

- Keep yourself organized and in charge of your schedule and will avoid any surprises due to a holiday weekend or a personal event.

- Plan ahead for the workshops you desire and vacations you want to take. Take them when the majority of your clients are also doing vacations and you'll miss fewer teaching sessions.

- Use an online scheduler as a way to see what you'll be making each week and plan accordingly. Having a budget isn't a new idea but adjusting to your new Pilates economy might be.

YOUR friends and family will hopefully be excited to support you, train with you and help you as you do your program, and when you're done. Ask them for some social media promotion to announce your completion. They offered their bodies to your practice and will have experiences to share with their friends and coworkers. Friends and family members are great to bounce marketing or business ideas off of, or practice new exercises and cues. You will be busier than ever, especially if you still have a safety job, and even after you've transitioned to full-time teaching, your schedule might be less available for social time. While the hours might be similar to your apprenticeship, the demand on your eyes, voice, and mind is different. Let your friends and family know the days that are better for you to spend with them, so they still feel loved while you get to do what you love.

In Amy Spencer's book, *Bright Side Up,* she talks about asking your 100 year old self what to do. Your 100 year old self will have the best advice. Knowing where you want to go, and when you want to get there will help you set markers and goals for yourself. **Your ultimate goals will help you determine where you should teach, where you should continue your education and training; goals will determine your ideal clientele.** So go market to those clients, search out those workshops and set yourself up at those teaching locations.

WELCOME to your new career. Welcome to a job that you'll never consider a "safety job." Welcome to a job you WANT to do!

CHAPTER 12

Final Thoughts... Good Luck!

IN conclusion let me say this...Good Luck! There is not much worthwhile in this world that comes easy. This journey you're embarking on will test you but it will also teach you and inspire you. There will be days when you feel like you've got it. And there will be days when you feel like you just don't know everything you wish you did, or anything at all. There will be weeks and months your schedule will be so full you can't handle another referral and then there will be days and weeks when you wonder where did everyone go? But most days, you'll be left with the profound feeling YOU helped some-body that day. Perhaps you got them to do an exercise they thought they never could or maybe just that you enabled them to dedicate a whole hour to their health and wellness.

THE more you choose to learn about Pilates, the more questions you ask, research you do and the more you challenge yourself, the more this job will give back to you. Over the past 6 years as a teacher, I've developed my own guiding principles. I would like to share with you:

- Believe in the Work: Trust in the method that Joe Pilates created to give your client what they need. Progress clients not because you are bored with the routine or because you think they are bored but because it is appropriate for their practice. Never force bodies to do something they are not ready to do.

- Envision your Own Success: Make a plan for yourself and work it! If you want to teach 10 hours a week then mark your calendars and start finding bodies to fill those spots. If you want 30 hours a week then working 30 hours a week towards that goal will get you there. Even if you're not teaching, fill up those 30 hours marketing, prospecting, practicing...before your know it those hours will be filled with paying clients. See what you want for yourself and then fill in the map to get there.

- Listen to the Client: Whether you are an apprentice or a full time instructor listen to the client. What are they saying? What are they not saying? What is their body saying? The equipment saying? All these sounds (or lack of sound) tell us something. The more you listen the more you can hear. Being present with your client will take your client further and your career farther.

- Listen to the Experts: You don't have to do everything they say nor should you. But those who have been teaching Pilates for a long time probably have information that helps you or maybe they say something that confirms a belief you've had. Every client is different and learning from others allows you to grab different tricks or even throw several out. Listen but ask questions. Don't just mimic-- decide if information is valid or not and then figure out how you can use to best serve your clients.

- Focus on the task at hand: Be present be present be PRESENT! Its so easy to be distracted whether you are an apprentice or full time teacher. Pay close attention to the body in front of you or the session you're observing and you'll grow so much more. As an apprentice you'll see things and hear things that will be useful when you're teaching regular clients. As an instructor your clients will gain more with you paying close attention to them. The more your clients gain out of Pilates the more they will be doing Pilates with YOU.

- Connect to the Work: It's so easy to stop taking your sessions...don't! Take from others, teach yourself and take continuing education. Your clients and you will gain more from Pilates if you have it in your body as well!

- Do what you do best! Copying off your neighbor didn't always help on a test and it certainly won't help here. If you're best with certain people or certain times do those! Don't try to be any other Pilates instructor than the best you can be. If you want to be better at something you're not then go get that education and practice.

- Go with your Strengths: see above! You will feel confident in areas you are strongest then as you find your groove and your teaching grows so will your strengths.

- Never stop Learning: There is education built into each session you teach. Beyond that, there are workshops, conferences, books and your personal sessions. There are a variety of workouts out there. Keep your mind open to analyzing new things and see what you can use for future sessions, clients and your teaching.

CLOSE your eyes, see yourself at the end of your teaching program, see yourself in front of your first client, tenth client, teaching your thousandth session. This career can be everything you want it to be. GO TEACH!

Additional Materials

FIRST TIME CLIENTS

The first time you teach a potential client you'll probably be nervous, anxious or even doubtful. Stop. You're not trying to create world peace, it's just Pilates. They're coming to you to see if Pilates is the answer, what Pilates is and what a session with you is like. Be you and teach what you know they need. That's the simple answer. Now for the nitty gritty...

First impressions are very important. You have heard this before. It's true here. If you work for a studio, club or office and they schedule the client for you then depending on the studios protocol you might not have much "Pre" or "Post" session work to do. If you work for yourself then be sure you are professional. You respond to their calls or emails promptly. Confirm their first appointment with them at least one time. If they prefer phone do phone confirmation as well as an email, or vice versa. Clearly communicate how to get a hold of you best, your cancellation policy and make them feel welcome. Treat them as if they are already a client they just don't know it yet.

You should not assume potential clients know how to set up, pay or schedule sessions. Where should they park? What should they wear? Before seeing them give them the information they need no matter how obvious it may seem. This way they can walk into the studio prepared to take their first of many sessions with you.

If you can get information out of them before the session it's better for you to plan. It doesn't always work out that way but it is nice for you to find out ahead of time if they have an injury, condition or maybe they're pregnant. The more you know the better you can plan an appropriate session. Also, find out their fitness goals. Why are they there? What do they expect? What experience do they have? Knowing the answers to these questions not only gives you more information to better prepare it also gives you a window into where they are coming from. If they have been doing Pilates for years with a Classical instructor and you are more Contemporary or vice versa you'll want to let them know your style might seem different then what they're used to.

In person you'll want to review any information you received "pre" session. You'll be surprised how many people will say they are injury free then halfway through the session you find out they have a rotator cuff injury or a hip replacement.

During the session you before you start pulling out all the "flashy" exercises to wow them take the 'less is more' approach. Take the time to help them "get" each exercise and explain why that exercise is good for their goals and/or needs. While you might make your clients do less than five repetitions of an exercise for a first timer you can bend this rule. They are new to you.

Keep the client moving, make sure they are experiencing the exercise where they are supposed to. Also, tell a client what you're seeing their body needs. They probably have no idea their right shoulder rounds forward or that they hike their hip up even when lying down. **You telling them what you see and giving them exercises to balance them out will show them how knowledgeable you are!**

During the session as you teach a client a new exercise, let them know how that exercise will help them with their fitness goals or their body's needs. Reminding clients of the goals they came in wanting to hit throughout the session and enables them to see how Pilates with you will help them hit these goals. By the time the session is over, if someone has been feeling Pilates in their body for an hour and hearing how it will help them achieve their goals, of course they will want to work further with you! Remind them what you saw their body needed. Isn't it great that Pilates can not only hit their goals but balance their body as well?! Instead of asking them what they think or if they are coming back. Tell them how often you need to see them to get them the results they are looking for. **Yes, I said TELL them.** You are their future trainer, you have a plan for them. Be confident in what you know they need, give them the information and your price card and set them up for their next session. Sure, they might say they'll get you or they need to think about. Tell them tha and you'll follow up with them to see how they are feeling and if any questions arose.

Whether they loved it, hated it or just seemed 'overwhelmed' always follow up with a phone call or email. Stay professional all the way through. A 'no' today could be a 'yes' next month. Or, they might not be able to fit it in but if a friend asks them where they can find an instructor if they'll remember you and refer their friend to you.

It's important that just like your 'elevator speech,' you don't shy away from the 'close'. Be confident. Be clear and then keep in mind you most likely will not convert every first timer into your schedule. But, the more you do them the easier it'll get. The more you connect with the client the better. Often times potential clients are buying Pilates with You before they're buying Pilates. It take many people at least 6-10 sessions to 'get it'. Get them to get you and then you'll have those sessions to help them get the method.

Much of what should be done during a session might seem like a given but keep these following tips in mind! They work, if you work them!

During the session be sure to:

- Have a questionnaire and use it!

  o Use it to find out past bone breaks, surgeries, general aches and pains, tightness or limitations.

Can they touch their toes? Lift their arms over their head?

o Do they workout? What do they do for workouts? How often do they workout? What are their goals? When do they want to hit them?

o Don't have them write these answers out for you. It's not the doctors office. You write them down, you ask them and you ask follow up's or share an experience that you had so they hear you heard them, understand them and are ready to show Pilates to them!

• Look them in the eye! If you're not a very outgoing person this can be challenging but it makes a difference. As a Pilates instructor you spend much of the session looking at the clients body and what its doing. During this first session welcome them making eye contact. When doing the questionnaire look at them when they are talking don't just look at your sheet. Make sure they see you are paying attention to them when they are talking. They are not just another "body". During the session when teaching them an exercise take extra time to look them in the eye when explaining why you chose the exercise for them or when they are telling you where they are feeling it. If you were having coffee with this person would you be looking at their body or their face?

- Future Phrases: While you are teaching them give them a map of where an exercise can go "next time" or "after several sessions" and "once you're able to do _____ then we can _____." Remember they are new to you and maybe even new to Pilates. They need to know that the exercises have progressions. Where can they go? Think about how intriguing this is. When you were learning for the first time you had no idea how many possible exercises there were or variations. As you found out didn't you want to do Pilates more and Pilates better so you could get to those next variations and exercises? Talking about progressions also implies they will be working with you in the future, well beyond this first session.

- What are they juggling?: If you see a female client with one hip hiked up higher than another ask her if she carries her child on that side. Or a client who comes in with rounded shoulders and slumped posture. Do you work mostly at a desk? Find out what they do in their daily life! Pilates isn't just another way to get fit but a way to balance their body. They probably have no idea that they show signals of a busy or stressful life all over their body. You will see it and use Pilates to help them have a place to come and leave that world behind if only for an hour.

- You, only better. Tell clients how Pilates can help make the activities they're currently involved in more effective! How refreshing for them to know they don't need to give those up. Even if the activity is what causing their imbalances, aches and/or pains, let your client know Pilates will allow them to do what they love even better!

Name:	
Goals:	
Start Date:	

CADILLAC	SESSIONS								
	1	2	3	4	5	6	7	8	9
LEG SPRINGS									
FROG									
CIRCLES									
WALKING									
BEATS									
BICYCLE									
SIDE LEG SPRINGS									
PUSH THROUGH BAR									
PUSH THROUGH									
FLYING EAGLE									
SHOULDER PRESS/TRICEPS									
TOWER									
ONE LEG TOWER									
SHOULDER ROLL DOWN									
MONKEY ,									
PRESS DOWN SIDE									
MERMAID									
TEASER									
CAT STRETCH									
COMBO									
SWAN									
REVERSE PUSH THROUGH									
OTHER									
BREATHING									
SPREAD EAGLE									
PULL UP FRONT									
PULL UP BACK									
HANGING									
HIGH BARREL									
SWAN									
SIDE SIT UP									
SHORT BOX									
ROUND									

FLAT											
SIDE TO SIDE											
TWIST AND REACH											
TREE											
BALLET STRETCHES											
FRONT											
SIDE											
BACK											
SWEEDISH BAR STRETCH											
HORSEBACK											
BACKWARD STRETCH											
ROLL BACK BAR											
ROLL BACK											
ROLL BACK ONE ARM											
CHEST EXPANSION											
LONG BACK STRETCH											
ROLLING IN AND OUT											
THIGH STRETCH											
AROUND THE WORLD											
ROLLING STOMACH MASSAGE											
AIRPLANE											
ARM SPRINGS											
PRESS DOWN											
CIRCLES											
TRICEPS											
STANDING OUTSIDE											
SQUATS											
ARM SPRINGS											
ROLL BACK BAR											
HIGH CHAIR											
PUMPING											
PUMPING ONE LEG											
STANDING PUMPING FRONT											
STANDING PUMPING SIDE											
PUMPING CROSSED OVER											
GOING UP FRONT											
GOING UP SIDE											
ACHILLES STRETCH											
PRESS UP FRONT											
PRESS UP BACK											
Footwork/hip stretch											

REFORMER	SESSIONS						
	1	2	3	4	5	6	7
FOOTWORK I, II, III, IV							
HUNDRED							
OVERHEAD/SHORT							
SPINE/LEG							
FROG/LEG CIRCLES							
COORDINATION							
ROWING							
SWAN							
PULL STRAPS							
T-SHAPE							
BACKSTROKE							
TEASER							
HORSEBACK							
SHORTBOX							
ROUND							
FLAT							
SIDE							
TWIST & REACH							
TREE							
LONG STRETCH							
DOWN STRETCH							
UP STRETCH							
ELEPHANT							
LONG BACKSTRETCH							
STOMACH MASSAGE I, II, III, IV							
TENDON STRETCH							
SEMI CIRCLE							
CHEST EXPANSION							
THIGH STRETCH							
KNEELING ARM SERIES							
MERMAID							
CORKSCREW/TICK TOCK							
BALANCE CONTROL							
LONG SPINE MASSAGE/LEG CIRCLES							
KNEE STRETCH SERIES							
ROUND							

MAT	SESSIONS						
	1	2	3	4	5	6	7
HUNDRED							
ROLL UP							
ROLL OVER							
SINGLE LEG CIRCLE							
ROLLING LIKE A BALL							
SINGLE LEG STRETCH							
DOUBLE LEG STRETCH							
SINGLE STRAIGHT LEG							
DOUBLE STRAIGHT LEG							
CRISS-CROSS							
SPINE STRETCH							
OPEN LEG ROCKER							
CORKSCREW							
SAW							
SWAN/PREP							
SINGLE LEG KICK							
DOUBLE LEG KICK							
NECKPULL							
JACKKNIFE							
SHOULDER BRIDGE							
SPINE TWIST							
SIDE KICKS							
TEASER							
BOOMERANG							
HIP CIRCLES/CAN CAN							
SWIMMING							
LEG PULL FRONT							
LEG PULL BACK							
KNEELING SIDE KICKS							
SIDE BENDS/TWIST							
MERMAID							
SEAL							
PUSH-UPS							

WUNDA CHAIR	SESSIONS						
	1	2	3	4	5	6	7
FOOTWORK I, II, III, IV							
PUSH DOWN							
PUSH DOWN ONE ARM							
PUSH DOWN BEHIND							
PUSH DOWN KNEELING ON TOP							
PULL UP							
PULL UP SIDE							
MERMAID ON TOP							
MERMAID KNEELING							
MERMAID ON FLOOR							
PRONE ARM PRESS							
PRONE ONE ARM PRESS SIDE							
LOW FROG							
LOW FROG ONE LEG							
PELVIC LIFT							
CAT STRETCH SITTING							
CAT STRETCH STANDING							
SPINE STRETCH FORWARD							
TEASER ON FLOOR							
TEASER ON TOP							
LEG PRESS FRONT, SIDE, BACK							
BACKWARD ARMS/TRICEPS							
SITTING MAST							
MOUNTAIN CLIMB FRONT, SIDE, BACK							
BALANCE CONTROLE FRONT, SIDE							
SWAN							
TWIST							
TENDON STRETCH							
TABLE TOP							
GRASSHOPPER							
PUSH UP I, II, III							
WALL							

SMALL BARRELS	SESSIONS						
	1	2	3	4	5	6	7
ARC BARREL							
FROG							
CIRCLES							
WALKING							
BEATS							
SCISSORS							
BICYCLE							
HELICOPTER							
ARM LIFTS							
ARM CIRCLES							
OTHER							
SPINE CORRECTOR							
STRETCH WITH BAR							
SIDE SITUP							
TEASER							
HIP CIRCLES							
SHOULDER BRIDGE							
CIRCLES ONTO THE HEAD							
GRASSHOPPER							
SWIMMING							
ROCKING							
SWAN							
OTHER							
PED-A-POLE							
UP - DOWN							
CIRCLES							
TRICEPS							
CHEST EXPANSION							
KNEE BENDS							
SWIMMING							
CENTERING							
OPPOSITE CIRCLES							
CHEST EXPANSION SQUAT							
ONE LEG KNEE BENDS							

PRIVATE SESSIONS

	PER SESSION	PROGRAM PRICE
1 Private	$	$
5 Privates	$	$
10 Privates	$	$

DUET SESSIONS
Two clients, price per client

	PER SESSION	PROGRAM PRICE
1 Duet	$	$
5 Duets	$	$
10 Duets	$	$

SEMI-PRIVATE SESSIONS
Three or more clients, price per client

	PER SESSION	PROGRAM PRICE
1 Semi-Private	$	$
5 Semi-Privates	$	$
10 Semi-Privates	$	$

*All sessions have a 24 hour cancellation policy. Anything cancelled or rescheduled after 24 hours prior to session will be charged full value of the session

REFERENCES

Return to Life and Your Health by Joseph H. Pilates
Bright Side Up by Amy Spencer
Yahoo Contributors, Elona Sherwood

WEBSITES

www.alternativebalance.com
www.citysearch.com
www.facebook.com
www.forrestpilates.com
www.giltcity.com
www.godaddy.com
www.goldstar.com
www.groupon.com
www.hootsuite.com
www.ideafit.com
www.lvingsocial.com
www.pilatesmethodalliance.org
www.powerpilates.com
www.socialbakers.com
www.square.com
www.twitter.com
www.ucis.gov
www.yelp.com

CPSIA information can be obtained
at www.ICGtesting.com
Printed in the USA
LVIC04n2312131015
458175LV00001B/2